office mate

The Employee Handbook for Finding — and Managing — *Romance* on the Job

Stephanie Losee and Helaine Olen

Adamsmedia
avon, massachusetts

The authors wish to acknowledge that some names, identifying details, and characteristics have been changed to protect the lovelorn (and the formerly lovelorn).

Published by
Adams Media, an F+W Publications Company
57 Littlefield Street, Avon, MA 02322. U.S.A.
www.adamsmedia.com

ISBN 10: 1-59869-330-1
ISBN 13: 978-1-59869-330-0

Printed in Canada.

J I H G F E D C B A

Library of Congress Cataloging-in-Publication Data
Losee, Stephanie.
Office mate / Stephanie Losee and Helaine Olen.
      p.   cm.
Includes index.
ISBN-13: 978-1-59869-330-0 (pbk.)
ISBN-10: 1-59869-330-1 (pbk.)
1. Mate selection. 2. Dating (Social customs) 3. Single women.
4. Sex in the workplace—United States. I. Olen, Helaine. II. Title.
HQ801.L65 2007
646.7'7082—dc22
2007025299

This book is available at quantity discounts for bulk purchases.
For information, please call 1-800-289-0963.

For our Office Mates-turned-husbands
. . . of course

Acknowledgements

We're grateful to everyone who told us their stories of finding love on the job. We'd name names, but some of you asked for anonymity. Numerous others generously shared their expertise, including Harriet Brand, John Hourigan, Pam Anderson, Esther Perel, Janet Lever, Andrea Phillips, Alan Deutschman, Amy Dickinson, and Michael Cohen.

We are grateful to our agents, Lauren Pearson and Joe Regal, for seeing the potential in this project when it was a page-long query letter. At Adams, we'd like to thank our talented editor Jennifer Kushnier, Beth Gissinger, and Karen Cooper. Kudos to Lynn Goldberg and Laura Pillar of Goldberg McDuffie Communications. We also want to give a shout out to all who advised us on the book biz.

Office Mate would not exist if our husbands had not been friends long before they knew either of us. So we'd like to thank our in-laws, Ron and Bunny Unger and Howard and Sylvia Roshkow, for deciding that their younger sons would be a great friendship match many years ago. Last, we are indebted to our children, parents, siblings, and good friends, all of whom gave up something, sometime, to make the completion of this book possible.

Contents

contents

FROM THE DESK OF

Helaine

I wanted his office.

I know this doesn't sound like the typical, starry-eyed beginning of a story about getting to know the man with whom one recently celebrated one's sixteenth wedding anniversary. But it's true. At the time I met Matt my life seemed defined by its lack of space. Tiny cubicle at work. Cramped third-floor walkup shared with my agoraphobic roomie and her two rabbits. Rush-hour commutes so jammed that a subway conductor would warble over the train's crackly loudspeaker, "We're all crammed in like sardines, we're all crammed in like sardines . . . " to the tune of "Hi Ho Cherry-O."

But Matt, my future husband, had a private space. Inexplicably, and unlike the rest of us overworked and underpaid editorial assistants, he had an actual office with a door where he could get away with combing the sports pages of every New York daily and engage in raucous long-distance phone chats with former college buddies, leisurely takeout lunches, and—this we found particularly galling—the occasional nap. All this while the rest of us, stranded in a makeshift hallway, did our best to avoid getting nailed by mailroom carts and speedwalking executives.

So I took action. Speaking on behalf of my fellow editorial assistants, I knocked on Matt's door and demanded a few minutes of his time. But before I could get around to delivering the speech I'd prepared in an effort to guilt-trip him into handing over his junior executive digs to a more worthy occupant, a weird thing happened. I found myself laughing.

First, there was the hilarious collection of awful manuscript pages he'd read and then taped for posterity to his wall; contrary to my suppositions, he did do some work. One featured a phrase so ludicrously clunky that Matt had challenged his colleagues to define exactly what it meant, with the winner getting a free lunch.

Then there was the charming, self-deprecating, "you caught me" way he admitted that yes, he did occasionally use the office for napping. But, he added, always in his chair. The office's small love seat was too crowded with manuscripts to allow for a truly relaxed snooze.

It seemed like years since I'd had that much fun just talking with a member of the opposite sex. My last date had been with a guy who told me all about the various twelve-step programs he was in. Programs, plural. When I returned to my cubicle my fellow editorial assistants were all poking their heads over theirs, demanding the dish on this much-anticipated showdown. "We're going out for drinks after work next week," I told them. "I'll ask about the office then."

A year later, after I changed jobs, I found myself missing my office mate. A lot. Soon, we were sharing a workplace again. Permanently. Some people would call it "home."

For years I attempted to help deliver my single friends into my wondrous married state. There was only one problem: my fixups went nowhere. Occasionally a woman would be interested in a second meeting with one of my picks. But the men were another matter. One guy waited three full months to call back my girlfriend. I swore off matchmaking for good after that.

But people were still asking for my help, inexplicably. So I went back to the drawing board. I had thought my story was unusual, but when I took a look at the marriages of my friends I realized that more than half had met at the office. And they weren't always obvious connects. There was the television writer and the costume designer. The Human Resources professional and the banker. The aspiring producer and the key grip. One advertising pal even shacked up with her intern.

None of these people began dating the day they met. Sometimes, in fact, it took them years to exchange more than a handshake. Many had become friends first, consoling each other through other breakups with other people. There was only one thing they all had in common: the luxury of time.

I thought about Matt. I knew if I had met my husband at a bar—well, I wouldn't have. He just wasn't that type of guy. If we had seen each other's profile on Match.com, both of us would have likely clicked "next." See for yourself:

Helaine . . . . *Matt*
Messy . . . . Neat
Politics. . . . . Yankees
Honest to the. . . . . Diplomat
point of tactless
National Public Radio . . Alternative rock
Barely watches TV. . . . . Film and TV writer
Shopper. . . . . Wears same three outfits repeatedly
Likes to travel . . . . Considers next block foreign turf

The odds of us both discovering we thought *I, Claudius* was the best television ever (well, until *The Sopranos*) over drinks was pretty miniscule. More likely, my husband would have dismissed me on the spot for chronic lateness. And I would have yawned if he mentioned baseball, just as I do now. So the next time someone approached me about how to get a date, I suggested they take a good look around their office. A really good look.

My success ratio soared. And I had done nothing but tell the truth: When it comes to finding love, there's no place like the office.

FROM THE DESK OF...

Stephanie

Before my husband Tom became my husband, he became a noun.

My single girlfriends thought he was the ideal man, and they wanted one, too. "How do I find a Tom?" they would ask. I told them to do what I did: look for a Tom at the office.

He was not my first office relationship. Before I found him I kissed two office frogs. First there was Jaz, an artist from the wrong side of the tracks who played guitar and sang like John Mayer. Then there was Tony, a much older man who looked like an Italian soap star. And finally I met Tom. Just Tom in those early days, not "a Tom."

Before I go on I should probably mention that I am a nice girl. I didn't intend to become an office serial dater. All I wanted was a boyfriend, and when I graduated from college there were none to be found. I was homeless and jobless, so I moved back in with my mother and stepfather. This was a barrel of laughs. I spent all of my waking hours either at work or commuting back and forth from my childhood home on Long Island to my job in Manhattan, a nearly three-hour daily round trip. Once home I would eat dinner and collapse into bed. Very sexy.

My mother suggested I join the youth group at the Manhattan branch of my childhood Episcopalian church, but I was not very churchy. A cool honorary aunt I had grown up with thought she had a better idea. She got me on the mailing list of a group of swank young Manhattanites who threw parties around the city, which sounded really promising. It turned out that the fee to attend the first evening was enough to pay for dinner for two at a four-star restaurant. Not that I would have had the nerve to walk into an event like that by myself, even if I had the funds.

My office, on the other hand, was filled with men. There was Jaz the artist, of course, and Tony the looker. Post-Tony, I had my eye on Rink—short for Ringland. As only someone called Rink could be, he looked like a model in a J.Crew ad. Guys like Rink did not normally go for me other than as a friend, and this Rink was no different. Rink introduced me to the new guy, who turned out to be Tom. Within moments I could tell that Tom was indeed that into me, which made him not in the least bit interesting. He was shorter than I was, for one thing, and he kept wearing this cream linen jacket that looked about two sizes too big for him. Also, he made bad jokes. Eighth grade–type bad jokes.

But the funny thing about the office is that you're forced to spend a lot of time with members of the opposite sex you'd have (wrongly) rejected in a hot second if you met them in a bar or on a blind date. It turned out that Tom had just gotten his MFA in creative writing and had already accomplished things in that arena that I had only dreamed about. And unlike Helaine and Matt we had dozens of things in common, among them virtually identical childhoods and markedly similar expectations. Tom and I became friends, and then best friends, and then we kissed one night when I went over to his place to watch my favorite show on his good TV. Six days later he asked me to marry him for the first time. I laughed it off. But eventually I said yes. And that's when Tom officially became "a Tom."

I started telling all my single friends who asked me that they should look for love in the office. They were appalled. Fine, I said, be appalled. You can surf the Internet and hook up with complete strangers. You can let some dude in a bar pick you up. But you can't turn to that cute man in the cubicle next to yours—the guy you know really well, the guy you've been working with for months, the guy who's been vetted by Human Resources—and let him know you're interested because it's appalling? At the very least you may find yourself a good friend. Maybe even a lover. And if you're really lucky? A Tom.

Introduction

Once upon a time, it was easy to meet a potential date. In school they were everywhere. *Everywhere.* But now you're out in the real world and you are wondering what happened to all of them. You see couples around every corner. They seem happy. Bully for them, but what about you?

Your mother can't understand why you're having so much trouble. She certainly had no trouble meeting your father.

So you go to a bar. Nothing. You get a friend to fix you up on a blind date. Yawn. The Internet never seems to lead to anything long-term—at least, not for you. The new relationships you do hear about are thoroughly random—your best friend says a hot young British actor just tried to pick her up on a street corner. It feels hopeless. You wish you had stuck with your college sweetheart. He wasn't so bad.

We've been there. Helaine was once dragged to a singles event at a local synagogue. She walked out after some guy pulled her long braid and asked if it would ring a bell. Stephanie was so bereft of postcollegiate possibilities that she started calling her guy friends from school—the ones she wasn't attracted to and had previously dismissed—and asking them to lunch hoping for a spark. She knew she had reached the bottom of the barrel when she found herself dining with a guy friend who used his face to inch his glasses back up his nose every few seconds.

But we saw the light, and it was a fluorescent bulb hanging over the cubicle of an attractive single. Both of us met our husbands on the job, and we're here to make the case for love in the workplace. Yes, we know that there is still a mighty stigma attached to meeting a mate where the boys really are. Business consultants routinely urge—or rather, beg—their clients not to engage in it. The consequences are too harsh. You won't be taken seriously ever again. You could lose your job, your reputation. It's too disruptive to workflow. You can leave yourself open to harassment or charges of harassment. And if you insist on doing it anyway, in God's name don't do it with a superior, they say. Or a subordinate. Or anyone who can be viewed as not exactly on your level. In fact, don't do it at all. Just don't do it.

Barbara Reinhold, a professional career counselor, just about summed up the opposition, when she said, "Smart women today owe it to themselves to keep their reputations squeaky clean and to work short enough hours to leave time for finding their romance outside of work, rather than in it."

But we think office romance has gotten a bad rap. We think its time has come. In fact, the greatest pool of potential mates is not online, not in a bar, and not on a blind date. It's in the office, and the office is the village, the town square, of the twenty-first century. The men and women we interviewed for this book seem to agree:

"When you meet someone in the office you get to see how they manage themselves and other people in a wide range of situations."
—Joyce

"The nice thing about dating someone from work is that you know them and you know what you're getting into." —Isabelle

"Your passion for similar work gives you something in common that goes beyond the initial sexual sizzle." —Ted

"I think the sense of having a basis of friendship first makes things a lot easier." —Belinda

"Fewer topics are touchy because you know you can disagree and it's okay; after all, you do it every day at work and it's not a problem." —Lee

"If I didn't date people I worked with, I would never have had a date. That's the reality for a lot of people. Everyone I know is through work." —Taffy

The most effective place to find a steady is where most of us spend the majority of our days, be it at an office park or the Parks Department. We use the word "effective" deliberately: studies show that between 20 percent and 40 percent of those who date an office colleague end up in what surveyors like to describe as a "committed long-term relationship." Why would you want to unilaterally shut yourself off from the most likely forum you have for meeting a mate—or even just a date?

In *Office Mate* we'll explain why the office has become the new town square, and then we'll show how successful it is in making "committed long-term relationships" that work—and we've got the statistics to prove it. You'll find out exactly why the Human Resources department has just become your new best friend. We'll explain how the dynamics of the workplace force you to play hard to get because you *are* hard to get, not because you're playing games. No more Rules Girl. You'll learn why the sheer amount of time you have to get to know your colleagues plays such an important role in helping you find the right partner in a way that's almost impossible in any other setting.

Unlike other dating and advice books, we won't be asking you to change yourself—not one bit. Nor is there trickery involved, no following of stringent self-imposed regulations designed to manipulate the opposite sex into happily-ever-after. We want you to be yourself, but more open to the possibility of finding true love where you've always been told not to look for it.

Offices, as it turns out, are good settings for happy accidents. We'll talk about the fact that your office pals might know you've made a connection before you do. That person with whom you have nothing in common—are you so sure about that? And while you're at it, you might also look twice at people from your previous office. Worried about Human Resources? Don't believe that old saw about HR being militantly opposed to dating between coworkers. At some companies, they're actively encouraging it. (We'll give you a few leads.)

We will also take a look at relations between superiors and subordinates, or just two folks on different status levels. Opposition to these inter-level relationships is actually increasing among Human Resources types weary of sexual harassment lawsuits, with 80 percent saying they should be firmly off-limits, up from 64 percent in 2001. But if you're interested in a colleague in your department, or someone up *or* down the ladder from you in another department, coming out of it with dignity (and possibly a life partner) is a matter of conducting yourself with grace and style, courtesy of the strategies you'll find in these pages. We know too many such relationships that worked out well to tell you to not go there.

What if your office is truly a washout? Herein you'll find suggestions about how to leverage your profession to find dates, regardless of the structure of your office. Yes, this might mean it's time for a new job (if your office is that stagnant, there might well be other things not working for you there, too), but there are less extreme measures you can take, including joining and regularly participating in professional organizations, finding opportunities to leverage your work skills by speaking or teaching, and strategically dropping in on your friends at *their* offices right around quittin' time.

Lastly, we'll tell you how to navigate the shoals of disaster, to make sure breakups and lusty supervisors don't derail either your job or your career.

Throughout the book we'll offer suggestions to help you conduct yourself with deliberation in office romance situations where most people act now and wince later. You ask, we answer:

- How do you indicate to a sexy associate that you're interested in a strategic alliance?
- Can you tell if someone is an office mate or office waste?
- Does every office relationship have to be classified?
- Is your boss off-limits? Your assistant?
- How do you know you have more in common than the next big deadline?
- What do you do if an office mate goes postal postbreakup?
- Does your career go in the circular file if you date more than one person in your company?
- Should you shop your résumé if your company has no romantic prospects?
- Can you work together if your merger ends up permanent?

It's not as overwhelming as it seems. We found our one true office mate. Many other people have too. So can you.

PART 1

why work just might be the perfect place to find true love

CHAPTER 1

It Takes a Village to Make a Marriage,

and the Office Is a Modern-Day Village

You need a village to find love. And you have one—you just don't know it yet.

Let us explain.

In the olden days, your grandparents and their parents and their parents before them had a village. A place where they were born, grew to adulthood, married, raised a family, and died. Their "village" might have been a city neighborhood, a small town, an ethnic enclave, a church—what have you—but it was a physical community.

Everyone knew everyone else. The marriage part—nobody was living together in those days— happened with the support of a community of interested parties. *Very* interested parties. The village wasn't going to let the young folks go off half-cocked falling in love with bad characters. Granted, back then their view of an appropriate match was restricted to someone of the same color, ethnicity, religion, and socioeconomic class—not standards we embrace today. But the point is that your grandparents didn't have to wonder who or what they were going to encounter on a date. Someone in the equation knew where the potential husband or wife went to grade school and whether they came from a nice family.

Don't believe us? Consider how Helaine's grandparents met:

My mom's mom was a widow, raising two children on her own with very little money. A year after her tailor's wife died, a mutual friend suggested he look up my grandmother. The man I would always know as my grandfather thought this was a fine idea. He knew my Nana Sara as a wife and then a widow for more than a decade, and had always been impressed by the resourcefulness and good cheer she'd demonstrated in a trying and difficult situation. They were married. From then on they could frequently be seen strolling their neighborhood—the one my grandmother lived in her entire life—arm and arm.

So, how did your grandparents meet?

_____

_____

_____

Certainly none of us lived one hundred years ago, and not all of us know our grandparents' stories, but we are all familiar with a classic village romance. Remember Laura Ingalls Wilder's *Little House* series of books, based on true stories of her childhood on the American frontier? The series could have been called "Little House of Romance." Laura first spies her future husband, Almanzo Wilder, at the beginning of the sixth book, *The Long Winter.* As she gets to know him as a farmer and fellow horse-lover, he proves his worth by venturing forth in dangerous subzero conditions to buy grain for the hungry town during a relentless winter. In *Little Town on the Prairie,* Laura has more encounters with Almanzo, none of which appear to lead anywhere. In *These Happy Golden Years*, Almanzo begins to fetch Laura from her far-off teaching job to bring her home on weekends. The students call Almanzo "teacher's beau" even though he and Laura have not exchanged so much as a peck on the cheek. After her job ends, they continue to see each other around town and Almanzo finally starts taking her for recreational horse and carriage rides on Sundays. The long-suffering Almanzo is allowed to kiss Laura goodnight only after he proposes marriage, and even then he has to make sure Laura's family approves his plans first!

You, on the other hand, live in another universe from that of Laura, your grandparents, and even your parents. Chances are you don't live where you grew up; you're in a town you moved to because that's where you could find a job. If you live in a city, you might not even know the names of your neighbors in the apartments to the left and right. You can't. You're too busy working.

FAST FACT

In the early 1950s, surveyors interviewed more than 400 couples applying for marriage licenses in Columbus, Ohio. They discovered that 54 percent of the couples lived within sixteen blocks of one another when they first began dating.

You spend the majority of your waking hours at the office. According to surveys, more than 40 percent of employees log more than fifty hours a week. In *Bowling Alone*, the national bestseller that chronicles the decline of community in America, author Robert Putnam writes that between 1965 and 1995, the percentage of Americans who said they spent time in "informal socializing"—including visiting friends and attending parties—

on a given day declined from 65 percent all the way down to 39 percent. So how and when are you supposed to meet someone? Where's your community?

Hello? We just told you. It's at work.

Your colleagues often know more details about your day-to-day life than your family does. Your boss's wife might not know he thinks the sales rep from Chicago is way too cute, but you do. Just as your family may not know that you flew to Virgin Gorda last year for Thanksgiving when you told them you were stuck in town on a deadline. But your work friends knew all about it.

You can't hide from them—they spend more time with you than anyone else. They've seen you under pressure. They've seen you early, they've seen you late, they've seen you the day your pet died and the week your mother was visiting and sat for a week on your very last nerve. They saw you right after you got your first promotion and right after you failed to get your second—the one you thought you had all tied up. *They're* your community, your village.

They constitute the new town square, the place where everyone comes to gather and where everyone can see you. And just as the town gossips provided the helpful service of praising good behavior and ferreting out the bad, the office gossips do the same today.

FAMOUS "DATES" IN OFFICE MATE HISTORY

2000 Robert Putnam publishes the national bestseller *Bowling Alone: The Collapse and Revival of the American Community,* documenting the disintegration of social structures in the U.S. and the resulting isolation of Americans.

Office Romance Is Old-Fashioned Romance (Perversely)

It's not only the village itself that has relocated to the office. Old-fashioned courting rituals have followed right along. Love and romance are now conducted under the watchful eyes of busybody coworkers, who serve as the resident nosy neighbors. Rules regarding civilized behavior are enforced upon pain of losing one's job, marking it as very different territory from the Internet, which is the romantic equivalent of the lawless Western frontier. There is no workplace equivalent for blind dates and speed dating—slow and steady is the rule. Potential mates are given the luxury of time in a low-pressure situation (at least dating-wise) to take the measure of one another. Unlike the Chris Rock joke about which version of a person you encounter on a date, you are not meeting someone's "representative" when you get acquainted on the job. You are meeting the real deal.

True, if you meet the real deal at the office instead of at a bar and it doesn't work out, you'll have to see him after you break up. But remember, work is your village. Can you imagine somebody from your grandmother's home town discouraging her from going on a date with the young man down the street because they'd have to bump into each other all the time if it didn't work out? *Oh, the horror! Everyone in town knows the both of them—think of the gossip! Best hunt for a husband who lives in another town entirely to avoid such a mortifying outcome.*

Of course not. The fact that they grew up near each other, that they knew each other for years before going out—that was considered a good thing. The fact that they had similar interests and expectations that came from their similar upbringing—that was considered a good thing. The fact that they were likely to be careful with each other because of all the consequences to their standing in the community—that was considered a good thing. Just as it's a good thing in your office.

IM from IHeartTheInternet ✕

Isn't the Internet the modern-day village? Sure, we aren't interacting face-to-face, but we bond over politics, interests, hobbies, and proclivities, you name it. Why, I can make a "village" of people who think *Star Wars* is the greatest movie ever, so why would I mess up my workplace when I don't have to? Times have changed, you know.

Hearty, honey, we're not here to judge how anyone meets their sweetie. People meet in all sorts of places and in all sorts of ways, from blind dates to supermarket checkout lines to the coach section of an airplane. But if you had a honey you found on the Internet, you would not be reading this book. Read on.

Let's talk about the Internet. The Internet may be many things, but it's not the modern-day village of your dreams. Here's why. At first, Match.com and JDate and such sounded like the ultimate way to discover the ultimate person. Who needs friends and family to find and screen potential mates when you can do it yourself, choosing from an enormous pool of right-age, right-stage people who want the same thing you do? And all this while sitting happily and privately at your cozy home computer, clicking from prospect to prospect as if you were channel-surfing on TV.

So you joined a service. You picked someone. You sent an e-mail. You got an answer. Maybe you felt like you and this person understood each other. Then you met and discovered that the system actually encourages dishonesty. Think about it. A short guy is convinced no woman wants to date a man who's 5-foot-4, and why wouldn't he be? Tons of profiles specify no one under five-ten need apply. A 5-foot-6-inch woman who gets to know Mr. Five-Four might find to her surprise that he's the man of her dreams in spite of the fact that he can't quite look her in the eye. But she wouldn't have given him the time of day over the Net.

We're not bashing the Internet, all evidence to the contrary. Everybody knows a match made in Internet heaven. We're just saying that the Internet is not the village we were expecting, the one to restore our lost sense of community. The kind of community that spawns lasting relationships.

Misery-Inducing Activities You Avoid by Seeking Office Romance

- Speed dating
- Texting someone you've never met
- Responding to unsolicited e-mails containing dubious information from unknown quantities way across the Web
- Reading a potential date's profile on MySpace
- Googling a stranger
- Having sex with someone mere hours after meeting
- Begging friends for fixups

Socially at least, the workplace is an awful lot like college, but with a paycheck at the end of the week instead of a grade. Work colleagues, handled properly, make a similar dating pool to classmates. Colleagues are a group of people with shared interests, whose backgrounds have been vetted by Human Resources (the workplace version of the Admissions Office), and whose passions have drawn them to the same company in the same industry. Many a recent graduate has been ejected from the warm cocoon of senior year into the wide world to find a stunning mass of inappropriate dating material lurking in every dark corner. The office extends the collegiate cocoon into adult life, and when it comes to searching for a life partner, a nice protective cocoon might not be so bad.

IM from DogEatDog   **X**

What office are you hanging out in? Mine is no cocoon, it's filled with backstabbers and nasties. They're too busy trying to climb over me for a promotion to consider going on a date.

- -

Doggy, have you been to a singles bar lately? Or even better, on the Internet? Post an innocuous comment on a chatboard and you are likely to get attacked by someone going by the moniker Puppy-girl673. Just because the office is competitive doesn't mean you shouldn't make friends—romantic or otherwise—with your colleagues. Law school is competitive too, and you never hear anyone say not to date there.

The fact that work is competitive and mistakes have consequences is not a problem. In fact, it's the prime reason why couples engage in the more old-fashioned courting behaviors we mentioned earlier.

Meet Danielle. She wasn't looking for love when she joined a high-powered L.A. law firm—she already had it. Because long after she left Austin to go to law school in California, she was still dating her dependable college sweetheart. What did she need with a social life, either in law school or at the law firm?

She had the sweetheart. And she had Jake, the associate assigned to the same managing partner with whom she spent many late nights and long weekends head-to-head over legal filings. But after three years of school and *two* of ninety-hour weeks at the firm, the sweetheart went the way of her Texas accent. She wasn't going to date for a while; she needed a breather before getting involved again. At least, that's what all the men in the office assumed when they thought about hitting on her so soon after her breakup. That is, except for Jake. Formerly known for coming in on Mondays chatting about weekend conquests, he suddenly turned mum about what outside social life he was managing. He moved in on Danielle so fast that the competition never got a shot at her. He brought her dinners during all those late nights, took her out for drinks, and when their work was handed in, he walked her home.

When we say that the office lends itself to old-fashioned courting, we mean exactly what you think we mean. Getting involved with an office mate means you don't have sex right away. And that's a good thing for those seeking a permanent merger. Why? Couples who delay sex are more likely to find themselves committed to one another than those who indulge. You don't have to take our word for it. In the 1990s, researchers studying American sexual habits found that only 10 percent of couples who had sex within a month of meeting walked down the aisle together. Couples waiting more than a year? An astonishing 50 percent found themselves exchanging vows. When you get to know each other at work, a relationship and sex flow from everything that interests you about the person, not the other way around.

We're not merely saying that the office has become the new town square, so go ye and find partners within. We're saying

{ 11 }

more than that. The office functions *beautifully* as the new town square. The fact that everyone has so much to lose protects you, whether you're a man or a woman. That was part of the magic of the old kind of community, the flesh-and-blood village of yore.

Just as this kind of community helps to create marriages, it helps to support them. If you marry someone you met in a bar, or met on the Internet, the two worlds you come from often remain just that—two separate worlds. Your friends, his friends. Which gang do we hang out with this weekend? But if your partner is someone a bunch of your mutual friends know, your mutual community cares what happens to the two of you. If you falter, they might be there to remind you what brought you together in the first place, how much you have to lose. Just like the old community did.

The dynamics of meeting at the office can prevent you from making a mistake, too. Working in close quarters means office mates know not just the good but the bad *and* the ugly (or the dirty), as Liz found out.

WATER COOLER CONFESSION

"dirty laundry"

"I was all set to date this guy in my office. Larry was cute, funny, single. It was so obvious he was interested in me. He was always lurking around my desk. If I spoke up in a meeting, he supported my position. There was only one problem. Every Friday, he brought his laundry into the office. One of my colleagues discovered the truth: It turned out he was going to his mom's house on Long Island after work, and she would do his wash. And ironing. He's thirty years old and he can't pour his own Wisk? I could see it all too clearly . . . after the first kiss, he would hand me the detergent. I decided to take a pass." ◖

Those peeping neighbors of ages past wanted a bit of gossip, yes, but they also wanted validation. If they approved of your relationship in the first place, they wanted it to succeed. No one wants to be proven wrong, be it on a cow farm or at the cube farm.

Office Romance Is More Accepted Than You Think

If an office is a good enough place to spend the majority of your precious days, it must be a good enough place to find a mate. The majority of working people agree. We can prove it.

A 2005 British study found that more than 70 percent of workers have had a relationship with someone they met on the job. Thirty percent of employees said they met their future life partner at work. American career book publisher The Vault, which conducts a yearly survey on the topic, found similar results in the U.S. Their 2007 study revealed that almost half of respondents had dated someone in the office, with one in five admitting going on a date with a supervisor.

Careerbuilder.com also takes an annual look at the state of love on the job. Here are the latest numbers: As with The Vault's survey, almost half of all workers admitted to successfully finding love—or at least a few dates—among their fellow worker bees. An impressive one-third of these office mates ended up walking down the aisle.

Managers are certainly not immune to Cupid's arrow crashing through their corner offices. In 2003, the American Management

Association discovered that 30 percent of bosses admitted to office mating, with 44 percent of those pairings leading to wedding vows.

So what are you waiting for?

takeaways from chapter 1

1. Office romance has gotten a bad rap.
2. You need a community to meet a mate.
3. The workplace is the closest thing we've got to the community of yore—the village.
4. If you can spend the majority of your time at work, it's a good enough place to find a mate.
5. More people have dated someone at work than not.
6. If managers get to date in the office, then so can you.

CHAPTER 2

How the Village Is Built

Or Why You Should Love and Adore Human
Resources Even Though They're Always Sending
You All Those Annoying Memos

B efore the city and the modern job market,
there were the village and the matchmaker.
Obviously, life was different in the village of
old than it is for most of us today. To begin, the
village was all about stability. Not a lot of new
people flowed in and out of it, so everyone was
known to everyone else. As for work, people
didn't generally hunt for the career most suited
to their unique skills and abilities. They inher-
ited their position in life. That was good and
fine if your position was Liege of the Manor,
not so great if the post you were destined for
was scrubber of the Liege of the Manor's floors.
There was no upward mobility, but at least the
village couldn't fire you. As for love matches,
they were few and far between.

You've heard that part before. In those days,
marriage and childrearing were considered far
too important to be left to the young to figure
out for themselves. After all, you never know

what follies young people will bumble into when they're left to their own devices. Marital partnerships were about forming a stable economic unit. A productive unit. A unit that could survive in the cold, cruel world. It helped if their respective families got along too, to such a degree that many pairings were arranged by the families themselves—with the help of a matchmaker, of course.

Chances are the closest you think you have ever come to a matchmaker was the time you saw *Fiddler on the Roof* or *Hello Dolly!* on DVD. Traditional matchmakers don't seem to be much of a modern phenomenon. How could they be? They weren't in the business of putting people together based on the likelihood that the pairing would result in romantic love. They focused instead on economic prospects, family background, dowries, and perhaps general temperament. They wanted to create successful partnerships. There's no correlative in our modern era.

Unless you consider the typical Human Resources officer.

Human Resources looks at a job applicant's background. Not who your parents and grandparents were, certainly. They evaluate your qualifications for the job. They look at your educational and work history. They check your references. They frequently try to gauge your temperament and interests, to see if you will fit into the prevailing corporate or office culture. They even check credit scores, which amount to a modern-day dowry: Too low a score, and an otherwise-promising candidate often won't get hired.

In assembling this ideal team, Human Resources is also doing a pre-sort of people who work together in more ways than one. They are—however unintentionally—bringing together people with common interests, similar views, and comparable backgrounds.

IM from IHeartTheInternet   **X**

Um, hello, haven't you heard of the Internet? It also performs a pre-sort, and a lot more efficiently than HR in my view. If I want to meet someone interested in classical music, I can. If I want to meet someone who hates classical music, I can do that too. Human Resources isn't asking about my outside interests. They just care that I can do the job.

- -

Hearty, we're all for Internet dating. But, as we explained in Chapter 1, you are expecting strangers to tell the truth when they post their online profiles. There is no impartial third party—like HR—validating the veracity of each and every (or any, for that matter) profile.

Your ability and desire to do the job automatically gives you something in common with your fellow workers. Human Resources doesn't expend all that energy to put together a group of people who cannot possibly get along.

IM from CityGal   **X**

Whether HR puts together people well or not, I can tell you that at my company the Human Resource department cares about only one thing: our ability to work together. Not play together. It's not in their best interests for me to have a love life. It would interfere with the work thing.

- -

Gal, that's exactly our point. In trying to find people who will work well together at a particular company, HR is accidentally screening for romantic compatibility. We didn't say they were

---

doing it on purpose. Unless, that is, you're work-
ing for a dating service.

In other words, the lovely *accidental* result of HR's efforts is a society of like-minded and accomplished people housed for most of their waking hours together in close quarters. Who needs Yente and Dolly when you have your compadres in Human Resources?

Why Human Resources Is Dolly the Matchmaker Meets JDate

- They check references so you don't have to cyberstalk.
- They verify résumé items so you'll know he's telling the truth about graduating from Stanford.
- They attempt to make sure the applicant will be a good fit with the existing corporate culture, and maybe with you too.
- They might actually find out if he *is* an axe-murderer.
- They sponsor orientations and skills sessions where employees can meet one another (and, of course, learn a few things).

One thing we need to make clear at this juncture: we are not suggesting that you spend your first day on the job casing the joint for future conquests. Please. The beauty of the office is that it allows things to happen slowly, naturally, even glacially, perhaps without your being aware there is something to talk about—but we'll get to that in the next chapter. For now, let's face it: A group of people in the average office has more in common by far than the same number of people, for example, in a bar. The only thing people in a bar have in common is their desire to drink in public at a place where they feel comfortable. Not too solid of a jumping-off point.

Mark had a lot more to go on when he met Amelia.

WATER COOLER CONFESSION

"love wanted"

"We needed to fill a position in our department and my boss gave me the assignment of writing up the ad, explaining what the person should be able to do, the qualifications, and all that. I forwarded it on to HR, and they ran it pretty much as I wrote it. A friend of a woman named Amelia saw the ad and called her up. 'I know you aren't in the job market,' she told Amelia, 'but this ad is you.' I interviewed Amelia and we hit it off right away. She was fiercely smart and perfect for the job, so we hired her. From the beginning I was attracted to her but one or both of us was always dating someone else. Four years after we first met, I realized neither of us was with anyone, so I asked her out on a date. Actually, I asked her if it would be okay if I called her and asked her on a date. She said yes. It progressed very quickly after that." ◀

Case Study: Testing for Love

Insiders suspect the screening process for new hires might account for the startling marital success of employees at test-prep concern the Princeton Review. Getting a job at this company is a lot like going to a twenty-first-century matchmaker, with potential employees being asked to complete a series of exams and tasks to determine their compatibility with the company and each other. Future teachers are made to take a standardized test; those scoring below a certain level are not invited back. Then prospective teachers need to audition by teaching a faux class for five minutes. "They need to be engaging, compelling, and hold the attention of a classroom," says PR Director Harriet Brand.

Brand is known as the "curator of couples" for her archive of photos and letters from the more than three dozen happy pairs who have met at the company. Since the company is, at its heart, a teaching concern, it tends to attract people who are "dedicated, humanitarian, and want to help other people," says Brand. Less deliberately, it is attracting people of similar educational backgrounds. Off-hours socializing between employees is encouraged, and that—combined with the long hours many put in—is a guaranteed formula for romance. Finally, management is supportive of the outcome. Says Brand proudly, "Almost all our executive management team met their spouses at the Princeton Review." That includes the firm's founder and CEO, John Katzman, who calls the place "*Friends* on Steroids." He should know—he met his spouse when she took a job at the company. "It was the typical late night at the office and going out for a drink afterwards," he said.

More Companies That Play Cupid

1. *National Public Radio:* More than sixty employee-to-employee marriages to its credit.
2. *Genentech:* Pairings at this Silicon Valley biotech firm are so common there's a name for them: "Genen-couples."
3. *Oxygen Media:* So many couplings, some employees started referring to the offspring that have resulted from on-the-job romances as Oxygen Babies.
4. *Southwest Airlines:* Officials at the *Fortune* 500 corporation estimate that approximately 1,200 couples are working

for them at any given time—that's 2,400 people out of 32,000 employees. Southwest employees routinely cite the company's hiring process as the reason behind the prodigious number of workplace couples. When you are looking for certain personality traits, they say, it's inevitable that friendships—and sometimes more—will form between people in the group. "When you are spending the majority of your day at one location, things can happen," notes Pam Anderson, Southwest's manager of employee relations. Their stock market symbol, LUV, is widely thought to be an in-house salute to the number of marriages and other happy pairings that can be credited to its hiring decisions.

5. _____ (Write the name of your firm here—after you find the love of your life while working there.)

As if you couldn't tell by now, it's an absolute myth that all Human Resources professionals are uniformly opposed to office romance. Southwest Airlines is more a rule than an exception these days in its attitude toward workplace love. Sure, some firms remain opposed to workplace romance, but they are hard to find these days—about as hard as finding someone who doesn't like chocolate. After all, most Human Resources officials are human and understand we are not robots. Certainly their foremost concern is that you do your job with a minimum of fuss. But this means they are more concerned about how you handle your office romance than whether you are having one.

Still not convinced? Let's return to Pam Anderson at Southwest Airlines. "We're open to relationships between our employees," she says. "It's the right thing to do."

Is Love on the Job Good for the Bottom Line?

Office romance doesn't pay dividends just for you. Your company cleans up too. There is research to indicate that love on the job can be as good for the bottom line as it is for the heart. So these love-friendly HR departments aren't just being nice, they're being business-savvy as well.

That's right. Your romance might actually make your employer a few bucks.

There is some evidence to show that those who are in love with someone at their company bring, shall we say, an added passion to the workplace. If you fall in love with a coworker you've shaken up your daily routine. That can enhance your creativity and problem-solving skills, not to mention increasing your productivity, boosting your commitment to the firm, and improving your attitude. "Employees often channel romantic energies to work tasks," said Montana State University psychology professor Charles Pierce, who has studied the topic extensively. "They bring enthusiasm and energy to their work."

When British researcher Chantal Gaultier studied love on the job, she found that it was breaking up—not hooking up—that caused the biggest problems. In her surveys, workers admitted to decreased performance in the aftermath of an affair gone bad, leading Gaultier to suggest that employers come up with policies to support former lovebirds who remain workplace

FAMOUS "DATES" IN OFFICE MATE HISTORY

2004 The *New York Times* introduces its "Modern Love" column, a navel-gazing look at love in the millennium. The columns regularly generate heated Internet chatter.

colleagues. Her reasoning? Given that corporate workplaces are a "perfect playground" for office relationships, the least companies can do is to support their workers when romance goes awry.

Are there naysayers? Of course. Other researchers point to the long lunches and coffee breaks known to be taken by the newly smitten—as if employees smitten by people who work in different places have never committed either sin. More seriously, they cite the tension that can result when charges of favoritism or sexual harassment are tossed about. But since you are reading this book, we know that won't be you.

So go forward and fall in love—you just might be adding to your company's profits when you do. Unless you fall out again.

FAST FACT

In a 2006 survey, fewer than 5 percent of Human Resources professionals felt that office romance should be prohibited. Still not persuaded the average firm is not too worried about coworkers dating? Just 9 percent of firms surveyed had blanket bans on office relationships. More prohibit pornography in the office. Really.

What If You Want to Date Someone in the Human Resources Department?

After all, Human Resources personnel have weekends to fill, too.

Alas and alack, they are the shoemaker's children of office romance. Two tales published in the *New York Times*'s "Modern Love" column show how much harder both sides have it when one of them works in HR.

When struggling Kevin Cahillane turned up at an ad agency looking for a job, he passed his typing test only because the cute woman in Human Resources gave him an extra five minutes. After a few weeks he finally got up the nerve to ask her on a date—only to get drunk and fail to show up. But she was such a sympathetic soul that she arranged a stay for him in an alcoholism treatment clinic, made sure a job was still there when he got out, and later married him. Talk about getting the most out of your friendly personnel office!

Still, you might not want to get involved with someone in Human Resources if there's any chance you might get fired. In another essay, Sara Pepitone described how her relationship with a former boyfriend never recovered after she found out that he would be fired in a mass purge—before he heard it himself. "He really didn't want me to tell anyone that I knew before he knew," she recalled. "My landing a job in another department while he continued to flounder only increased the distance between us."

Do You Ever Need to Involve HR?

In a word, yes. Start by finding out your company's policy on the subject. Obviously you don't need to tell them about a flirtation or a one-night stand (though, for the record, we strongly discourage one-nighters in the workplace—see Chapter 14), unless you believe for some reason it could lead to a charge of harassment. Nor do you need to inform them about a date or two.

It's when you're on your way to becoming a serious couple that you need to figure out whether your firm's policy demands you disclose. As we said earlier, it's unlikely to be a blanket ban or a demand that you come in and register your relationship.

FAST FACT

The majority of firms have no comprehensive policy on inter-office dating. Surveys have repeatedly shown that less than a third have any written policy at all.

It's not that companies never get queasy. There is one relationship that stresses out even the most supportive firms. That's the boss-subordinate coupling. We'll address this in much greater depth in Chapter 12, but it is worth noting here that these relationships are almost always good for some major difficulty, which is why we suggest you run, don't walk, away from them. When an undeniable kinship strikes you and someone much higher or lower on the totem pole, however, we know you are unlikely to do that.

Recognizing the role HR plays in putting you elbow to elbow with all those intelligent, capable people does have its downside: you won't be able to complain about all the paperwork they fling at you anymore. Awareness does have its costs.

takeaways from chapter 2

1. Human Resources, in *Office Mate*-ese, translates to "matchmaker."
2. Human Resources professionals are rarely opposed to inter-office dating, contrary to popular opinion.
3. As invisible as they seem in the process, your friendly neighborhood Human Resources person is the first person you should thank when you find love at the office.

CHAPTER 3

Office Mate Orientation,
Or the Anti-Rules

In 1995, the hot dating advice book was *The Rules: Time-Tested Secrets for Capturing the Heart of Mr. Right.* It taught its readers how to nab a husband by playing *very* hard to get. As much as a woman might want to express her mutual interest in a man, she was supposed to return his phone calls seldom, if ever. In addition, women were instructed to pretend to be busy whenever a man expressed interest. This behavior was intended to provoke a man's hunting instinct and inspire him to chase. The Rules were sexist, rude, and offensive. By all rights, the book should not have been a bestseller. Except for one little detail: *The Rules* worked.

Why? Because unattainability is one of the most effective aphrodisiacs there is. It's a rare member of our species who values the things that come easily. Remember the Groucho Marx line, "I refuse to belong to any club that will accept me as a member"? That sentiment, unfortunately, applies to romantic prospects as well.

When we conducted interviews of workplace couples for this book, several themes came up repeatedly. It did not escape our attention that numerous couples mentioned that while one of them was gung-ho for a romance from the start, the other was not. Frequently it was the man who "knew" right away while the woman kept her distance—for months or even years. The man was forced to chase, and to wait. The product was a successful long-term relationship.

So the workplace, in our view, is the perfect laboratory in which to experiment with *The Rules* and see how you can benefit from them without having to follow them. Because why would you want to? We're feminists here. We thought we'd come up with a few non-rules. Call them the Anti-Rules. Some counter a particular Rule, and others repudiate whole clusters of Rules at once.

Office Mate Anti-Rule No. 1:
There's no need to attempt to manipulate men into chasing you.

If you're a once and future *Rules* girl we feel compelled to inform you that men are not stupid, no matter how hormone-driven. Contrary to what it says in *The Rules,* men can sense a game or agenda and—in our observation—don't often follow the script. But in the office, you're not playing games to lure someone into a relationship. You've got more important things to do—keeping your job, for one thing. It makes you hard to get, yes, but authentically so, not because you're adopting a fake persona. Here's why:

- You're genuinely worried about career suicide.
- You're genuinely worried about what will happen if you break up.

- You don't know him well enough to take the above risks and you won't know him a whole lot better for quite some time.
- You don't think he's your type, since he never would have passed the glance-across-a-crowded-bar test.
- You're competing with him for a promotion.
- You're worried he's not hard-driving enough to ever get promoted over you.
- He's one of your best pals and you don't want to screw up a perfectly good friendship.

None of the above is a bad thing. The fact that these worries keep you from jumping into an office relationship works for you on two levels—it keeps you from dating the wrong man and it heightens the interest of the right one. That's what *The Rules* were going for. What was Rule No. 1? Be a "Creature Unlike Any Other." And you were supposed to become that Creature by behaving as if you were unavailable. So congratulations, you're an instant Rules Creature. And it didn't take any deliberate game-playing to get you there. Just ask Elise and Andrew.

WATER COOLER CONFESSION

"a finished symphony"

"I met Elise when I won a national musician's competition. My prize was a national performance and Elise, an accomplished administrator, as a mentor for a period of time. She helped me gain valuable exposure and taught me the publicity ropes. I immediately fell in love. She was in her twenties, doing this bang-up job, and she was brilliant and beautiful. I very quickly thought this was the person for me. I kept coming up with reasons—legitimate ones—to call her office. Her staff knew how I felt and put my phone calls through immediately, but Elise just thought I was simply eager for her advice and was absolutely shocked when after a few months I finally asked her out to dinner. She came but informed me that she would never date a musician—she thought that two people who worked in the same industry would be a disaster. Who, she asked me, would we turn to when the pressures of work became too much? I said I understood but I stuck in there, following up over the next few weeks. Her office staff was completely supportive, and put my phone calls through right away. I sent her a half-finished composition and said I would only complete it when she relented. Finally a coworker interceded by inviting us both out to dinner without telling either of us that the other one would be there too. I've never pursued anyone or anything like that before or since." ◗

Office Mate Anti-Rule No. 2:
In the office, you don't have to pretend you're otherwise occupied to give the relationship time to develop.

Several of the Rules were aimed at slowing things down—the initial pace of the relationship ("Don't See Him More Than Once or Twice a Week"), the revelation of intimacies ("Don't Open Up Too Fast"), and especially the leap into bed ("No More Than Casual Kissing on the First Date" and "Don't Rush into Sex"). No need to impose any of this on a burgeoning office romance. At work you and your crush have nothing but time. And when you meet someone and you don't immediately begin to assess their potential as a possible date, you get to know them. That

FAST FACT

> A recent study found 22 percent of office romances began while colleagues were working together on a project and another 15 percent found love while clocking overtime.

was the best thing about the old times. And when you work together, you spend quality *and* quantity time together. You get to know each other without trying to get to know each other.

Is someone good in a crisis? You'll find out by charging toward a deadline. Drinks after work or Friday Beer-Thirties are much less loaded—they can just be drinks after work, not a prelude to a date. Ask Helaine: she still has the credit card receipt from the first time she and her future husband went out alone after work, since she saved it on the off-chance her accountant wanted it. Same with working late. You're together, it's the evening, you've got takeout, but it's not a date. It's overtime.

There is another hidden benefit to time. It restores the traditional mating dance—the old-fashioned one, the slow-moving one. And as the authors of *The Rules* noted, the traditional mating dance worked.

What about the subtle signs of a fine character that you would have no way to know about except by spending long amounts of time together, perhaps under trying conditions? Like these medical residents, Lorraine and Steve.

WATER COOLER CONFESSION

"skipping sleep"

"Steve and I were both residents; he was a first-year and I was a third-year. We worked every day, and every third or fourth day we'd work the night, so those were thirty-six-hour shifts. We were on different teams but on the same rotation, so we were together when we'd work the night shift. My first clear memory of Steve is seeing him walk down the corridor with this box of dim sum he'd bought for his team to eat for lunch. When you're working that hard, everything becomes about getting more sleep, so the time he took going out and getting that food meant he'd have to give up sleep. I thought, 'What a sweet guy.' Soon thereafter we were writing up our progress notes on the patients and he told me he played the piano. I said I'd love to hear him play. So our next night shift he showed up with this sheet music and took me to the auditorium of the VA hospital where we worked. It was about 3 A.M. and we should have been cat-napping. I was blissing out listening to him when the MPs came and told us we couldn't be in there. Soon after that a friend offered me symphony tickets she couldn't use and I said I wanted to invite Steve but I was too shy to ask him, so she invited him for me. That was our first date. We have two children and we've been married for nineteen years." ◗

The value of exposure to another person over time in making a love match cannot be overstated. Every other current method of meeting potential partners puts a premium on first impressions. A *Washington Post* story by Libby Copeland called "Picky, Picky" described the dreaded "Taquito Moment," referring to the instant when a person realizes he can't date a prospect because of a tiny non-negotiable detail. The term was named for an incident in which a man rejected a woman who otherwise interested him because she craved a lowbrow convenience-store taquito after an evening of bar-hopping.

The Taquito Moment is an example of something that bestselling author Malcolm Gladwell writes about in his book *Blink* called the "Warren Harding Error." Harding, it seems, was quite handsome. He looked so much like a leader that his handlers got him elected twenty-ninth president of the United States despite a thoroughly undistinguished political career. Not surprisingly, historians judge his time in office harshly, with some calling him the worst American president ever.

Gladwell calls the Warren Harding Error the dark side of making decisions based on first impressions. While Gladwell thinks snap judgments can often be right, he points out that we can't trust our judgment when it comes to outward appearances. We often give someone attractive more of our time when they don't deserve it, and someone less attractive the brushoff. That's bad in politics *and* love.

Time is the antidote to the Taquito Moment and the Warren Harding Error. But you knew we were going to say that. Andi and Vadim's story is a case in point.

WATER COOLER CONFESSION

"the patient russian"

"Vadim was a consultant who visited our office on business about once a week. He would just stand in the doorway to my office and smile. It got to the point where I would call my mom and say, 'That Russian guy is here again.' Other times he would telephone on 'business' but not have any to conduct. One day late in the afternoon, he came into my office and just started talking. He seemed reluctant to leave so I ended up asking him to come to dinner with me. We had a great time—we stayed out until four in the morning, shut down the bar. The next day I went out on a fixup and I realized I wasn't interested because of Vadim! At that point it was pretty easy. We just fell into dating. I think I was initially interested because at first I had all the power—he was just so into me. And, suddenly, I was just so into him too." ◗

Andi wasn't being a *Rules* girl by putting Vadim off. But the exposure she had to Vadim's sweetness, his personality—and yes, his ardence—showed her over time that he was the right man for her.

Office Mate Anti-Rule No. 3:
Don't date him if his actions in the office don't conform to your values.

One of the objects of *The Rules*' rules was to motivate the man to chase the woman, and to give him arbitrary tests he didn't know he needed to pass. One example was Rule No. 12: "Stop Dating Him If He Doesn't Buy You a Romantic Gift for Your Birthday or Valentine's Day." But we know a lot of women who are happily married to a lot of considerate men who don't happen to observe birthdays or Valentine's Day consistently. Maybe your needs are different. Maybe you need a man who will consistently sit down with you and make you feel better about a tough event in your day, not ignore all those nights in favor of the two that the *Rules* authors have decided are most important. What tells you whether a man can perform the kindnesses that are most important to you is time and exposure—not tests.

You can easily find out enough to know that this person you thought you were attracted to cannot fulfill your needs or is otherwise unworthy of you. And you don't have to endure the messy process of dating him for a while and then breaking up to find that out. Where else but in the old-time village did you get a chance to observe a person's character in action *before* you started dating? Workplaces offer unlimited opportunities to lie, cheat, obscure, finagle, and engage in outright criminal activity. Even if you don't observe the object of your crush in (felonious) action, someone who's been at your company longer likely has. All you have to do is ask the office gossip and the information will come a-pouring out. It's better than hiring a personal investigator. Or Googling.

Office Mate Anti-Rule No. 4:
No need to make any judgments based on first impressions—you can get all the impressions you want.

Rules girls didn't actually get to make judgments made on any impressions, first or otherwise. They weren't supposed to approach a man, so their impressions didn't matter. "The premise of *The Rules* is that we never make anything happen," write the authors, "that we trust in the natural order of things—namely, that man pursues woman." But *Office Mate* women have the chance to broaden their romantic playing field by taking first impressions out of the mix and enjoying such constant and substantive contact that their predating knowledge of a potential mate goes much deeper than with other ways of meeting.

We all know that opposites attract, but not on a first date. Office courtship can allow for so much time to get to know someone that those little traits that might really put you off during a first date ultimately become irrelevant. Cruising a dating site, would you really sign up to meet a jazz fan if you can't get enough of rap? Worse, you might find a profile of someone who really interests you but who claims he values neatness so much he would never consider dating a slob—and allow your untidy self to be dissuaded. Look how far off the mark Annie's first take on John turned out to be.

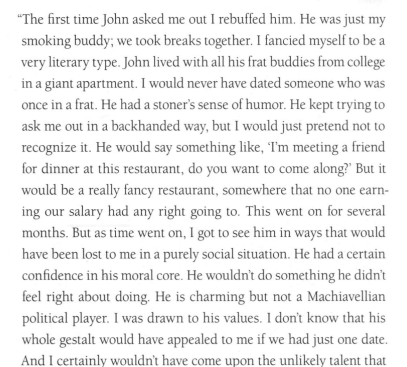

"the literati and the fraternati"

"The first time John asked me out I rebuffed him. He was just my smoking buddy; we took breaks together. I fancied myself to be a very literary type. John lived with all his frat buddies from college in a giant apartment. I would never have dated someone who was once in a frat. He had a stoner's sense of humor. He kept trying to ask me out in a backhanded way, but I would just pretend not to recognize it. He would say something like, 'I'm meeting a friend for dinner at this restaurant, do you want to come along?' But it would be a really fancy restaurant, somewhere that no one earning our salary had any right going to. This went on for several months. But as time went on, I got to see him in ways that would have been lost to me in a purely social situation. He had a certain confidence in his moral core. He wouldn't do something he didn't feel right about doing. He is charming but not a Machiavellian political player. I was drawn to his values. I don't know that his whole gestalt would have appealed to me if we had just one date. And I certainly wouldn't have come upon the unlikely talent that clinched the deal: when John showed me he could do Rubik's Cube with his toes, I knew I had met the right man." ◗

You're going to spend so much time with potential mates in the office that you'll quickly learn all the ways in which they're different from you. Some differences matter. Many don't. The ones that seem so important on a first date have a way of fading out later on—why let them get in the way of a beautiful more-than-friendship? As Helaine pointed out in her preface, she can't sit though a single inning of a Major League Baseball game, while her husband knows the roster of minor league teams few have heard about, much less followed.

After all, if a Matalin can marry a Carville and a Kennedy can marry a Schwarzenegger . . . .

Office Mate Anti-Rule No. 5:
Go ahead and look for someone like yourself—
now you have the chance to find him.

You're not a *Rules* girl, so you're allowed to look for this guy you want. You can even decide that you want him to be a lot like you. Like-minded people attract, yes—but not always on a first date. The key is in the phrase "like-minded." How long does it take to figure out that you and a potential partner are "like-minded"? All you can see at first glance is if you're like-aged, or like-looking. If he's built like you like 'em, if he dresses like you like 'em, you're attracted. Nowhere in there is the way a person thinks at the fore. How can it be? Like-minded doesn't factor into a first impression.

At work, watch his actions to see if he shares your values. Listen to him talk about what he does after work, on weekends, during vacations. Find out everything you want and take all the time you need. If your idea of romantic heaven is someone who wants to rent the same movie as you and watch it while sitting on your sofa, now's your chance. And one way to help that scenario to happen is to break Rule No. 2, "Don't Talk to a Man First (and Don't Ask Him to Dance)." If you love to dance, this is something you might like a potential office mate to know. And you might like to know if *he* loves to dance.

Office Mate Anti-Rule No. 6:
Be your everyday self.

Your potential Office Mate already likes your everyday self. It's not just your everyday mind that a potential office mate gets acquainted with. It's your everyday look, your everyday manner. When you start dating someone in the usual way, it's your evening look and your evening manner that's on display. What woman hasn't wondered if a man will still desire her without makeup, when she's wearing sweats and her hair is in a scrunchie?

Granted, you're not walking around in sweats at the office. But the office has a way of grinding us down to something way below a Saturday night look. There is a scene in the 1987 film *Broadcast News* in which Holly Hunter and William Hurt are at a dressy party together at a colleague's home when Hurt makes the mistake of observing that Hunter's character looks "so clean and pretty." When she asks him what he means by that, he replies, "Well at the office you always have this sort of *film* over you." Film or no film, it didn't seem to bother Hurt's character any. He pursued Hunter until she was forced to reject the possibility of a relationship with him after she was led to see something unethical he did on the job (see Office Mate Anti-Rule No. 3).

FAMOUS "DATES" IN OFFICE MATE HISTORY

2001 Ellen Fein, coauthor of *The Rules*, files for divorce after sixteen years, citing abandonment.

The office comes a lot closer to replicating the interactions you'll have over time with your sweetheart than dating does, you have to admit. You spend your days together, building something of value (or at least, we hope your work makes you feel like you're building something of value). That time has a lot to do with what it will take the two of you to create a life together. You'll have to deal with ups, downs, time crunches, long hours, finances, you name it. That's what much of your time in a relationship will really be spent on, isn't it? Especially if you end up raising a family together. How many long-term relationships go on feeling like a date—formal, wine-soaked, with candles and tree lights and wait staff?

The thirty-fifth and final rule in *The Rules* is, "Be Easy to Live With." That's a charming thought, and it's certain to attract a partner who hates a challenge, we'll give you that. But what if you're not easy to live with? What if you're, how shall we say, persnickety? Or overly chatty, or a bit short-tempered, or hateful until you get your coffee, or any number of other quirks? Which is to say, what if you're human? Better to date someone who knows this about you. Better to date someone who *likes* this about you.

takeaways from chapter 3

1. *The Rules* are a little silly. No surprise there.
2. To the degree that *The Rules* work, there's no need to follow them in an artificial way. The atmosphere of the office naturally causes you to be hard to get, not to act hard to get.
3. The ways in which the office inhibits you from acting on your attraction in a wanton fashion only works in your favor.
4. If a guy likes who you are in the office, he'll like who you are anywhere.

CHAPTER 4

You're in Good Company
(in More Ways Than One)

Let's play a guessing game. What do the following people have in common?

- Microsoft Chairman Bill Gates
- CNN correspondent Christiane Amanpour
- Barack Obama
- Meredith Vieira
- Julia Roberts
- Jennifer Garner
- Brad Pitt
- Angelina Jolie
- DeeDee Meyers, former press secretary to President Clinton
- Bruce Springsteen
- James Taylor
- Newt Gingrich
- Former G.E. Chairman Jack Welch
- Kate Spade
- Kate Winslet
- Cate Blanchett

Flummoxed? Unlikely, since you're reading this book. Yes, all these people, from CEOs to movie actors, met their current partner on the job, be it a movie set or a skyscraper. Which means that having an office romance is your chance to act like a star.

Some of these big names worked together directly; others met at industry functions. Either way, their experiences illustrate how office mating works, given the fact that they're high-profile people whose stories are known to many of us. Why wouldn't their stories be known to us—the consequences of the way they handle their workplace romances get splashed all over the pages of *People* magazine. So let's talk about some of the things we've watched celebs do over the years to introduce some of the ideas we'll cover in the rest of the book.

Prominent people are hardly immune to the highs and lows of meeting a mate on the job. In fact, they may be even *more* susceptible (or able to benefit) than the rest of us. One reason is that they are subject to a kind of isolation that is difficult to fathom. Imagine you're single and your name is Bill Gates or Brad Pitt. You've got a long list of romantic prospects. Women are clamoring to meet you. But many of them want to meet you for the wrong reasons—you're famous, or wealthy, or they want something from you. This is where the term "groupie" comes in. Not really marriage material.

There's another factor at play here. Unless they are careful, celebrities and other very important people can find themselves surrounded by sycophants, those folks who tell them only what they want to hear. Would you want to be the one to inform Bruce Springsteen, "Your new song sounds a little *too* much like Pete Seeger"? We didn't think so.

IM from NotEvenAlmostFamous   ✕

Pleeze. We all know celebrities are nothing like us ordinary people. They don't "work," not really. I'm sorry, but I don't buy the idea that a concert tour or a movie set is like my office. I just don't.

- -

NotEven, whether it takes place on a concert tour bus, on a movie set, or in an office building, when someone pays you to provide them with your expertise you're doing a job.

As with any other job, people on movie sets, on concert tour buses, or in the corner office find it nearly impossible to fake a persona. The usual rules will apply. The long exposure of a workplace atmosphere will force people to be real and get to know one another—an especially valuable gift for well-known people. Moreover, many prominent people have workweeks that put us pikers (logging a mere fifty- to sixty-hour week) to shame. Even if, say, famed CNN correspondent Christiane Amanpour wanted to meet her mate away from her job, it's unlikely to happen. How many hours does she have to herself, after all? Certainly not enough time to scour Internet dating sites, looking to see if some guy caught her fancy and was still listed as available. She had better things to do . . . like reporting on the collapse of the former Yugoslavia.

Amanpour met her husband, Jamie Rubin, the way that only she could. Rubin was the chief aide to now-former Secretary of State Madeleine Albright. CNN correspondent Amanpour was covering an Albright visit to Bosnia. On the plane trip from Washington, Rubin accompanied his boss to the back of the plane to meet with a few journalists. He and Amanpour exchanged a few significant looks and went out for margaritas alone later that night. The rest, as we say, is *Office Mate* history.

For celebrities, just like for us, the workplace is not limited to the actual place of employment. Both Amanpour and her husband were on an extremely high-end version of what could be termed a "business trip" when they met. Their paychecks came from two different entities.

Actors Harrison Ford and Calista Flockhart first met at the equivalent of a conference—in this case, the Golden Globe Awards, when Flockhart spilled wine on Ford's statue. Singer James Taylor was introduced to his current wife Kim Smedvig when he made a guest appearance at the Boston Pops; she was head of marketing and public relations for the Boston Symphony Orchestra at the time and in charge of arranging many details of his concert.

If you work in the same field, you don't necessarily need to share the same office—or even the same employer—to know one another through your work. Outside events can bring you together. Regular Joes might attend a conference in another city, whereas celebs might attend an event like the Academy Awards or jet off to an exotic foreign locale for filming. It's all the same thing in the end, although we admit the celebrity junkets are a tad more glamorous.

Celebrities Start Out as "Just Friends" Too

Also like us regular people, well-known folks can meet, become friends and nothing more—until suddenly, there's something more. Love that takes time has a chance to thrive when you're exposed to someone more than once because of a work connection.

Handbag designer Kate Spade first met future husband Andy while a student at Arizona State University, where the two worked together at a clothing store. Just friends—that is, until they both moved to New York City years later and met up again.

Another benefit of having the time spent at work is that you can use it to get over bad first impressions. Cate Blanchett and her husband, screenwriter Andrew Upton, were hardly a case of love at first sight. "He thought I was aloof and I thought he was arrogant," Blanchett has said of their initial meetings. "It just shows you how wrong you can be."

And the fact that work keeps throwing people together means first interactions aren't the only chance a couple has to move from interest to action. It gave actor Kate Winslet an opportunity to meet the man who would later become her husband.

Winslet met *American Beauty* director Sam Mendes in 2000 when she was separated from her first husband, assistant director Jim Threapleton. Winslet and Mendes discussed a project but didn't see each other again until months later at a barbeque. Winslet now says that she knew she was meant to be with Mendes from the moment they met, but she kept it to herself until bumping into him again. Within weeks, they were seriously dating. As she told *Parade*, "I believe in fate. We were meant to meet: Both of us from Reading, both born in the same tiny hospital, Dellwood. Then suddenly, years later, this totally gorgeous, sexy, talented man is in my life? That's fate."

The Celebrity Office Gang

Even celebrities sometimes need a helping hand before they can see what everyone else sees is going on between them. Why should we be surprised? Maybe whatever work ethic got them so well known makes them even less likely to see the potential office mate in the adjacent trailer, editing room, or limosine. *Today* show host Meredith Vieira certainly needed a push to get past her first impression of Richard Cohen.

When CBS news producer Cohen heard a woman's voice come through an audio feed into his New York City office one afternoon more than twenty years ago, he asked a coworker for her name and said, "I am going to marry that woman." Unfortunately, his first in-person meeting with on-air correspondent Vieira would be less than auspicious. Catching her watching *Looney Tunes* cartoons while on the job, Cohen said something less than complimentary about Vieira's journalism skills. She returned the compliment a few hours later while viewing a piece of his about a local political battle. The exchange of insults led, in true classic romantic comedy fashion, to a flirtation and friendship but didn't proceed any further until a mutual friend and coworker set the two up on a dinner date. Said Cohen in his 2003 memoir *Blindsided*, "We both had been married to the company for too long. Employers love you to death when it suits them, but they don't kiss back . . . . We knew there was more to life than we were getting."

When Pretend Feelings Turn Real

Celebrities are just as prone to make workplace mistakes as we are, elevating office waste to office mate and repenting at leisure, usually while reading stories about their marital mishaps in the tabloids. Anecdotal evidence suggests actors are more likely to do this than just about anyone else. The reason is not hard to figure out: when you're playing the role of someone in love, it is not too hard to begin thinking you actually *are* in love. When the part goes away, often the relationship does too.

Unfortunately for celebrities, this takes place in the public eye. Examples of deeply confused celebs include Ben Affleck and Jennifer Lopez, who met on the set of *Gigli*, and Jennifer Aniston and Vince Vaughn. They met on the set of *The Break-Up*, which has to be the worst omen in *Office Mate* history.

But don't despair. Many celebrated Hollywood relationships began on a film set and have persisted, seemingly happily. They include:

- BEN AFFLECK and JENNIFER GARNER
  Met on the set of *Pearl Harbor*; they began dating after working together on *Daredevil*
- JAY MOHR and NIKKI COX
  Met when Mohr guest-starred on Cox's series *Las Vegas*
- MICHAEL J. FOX and TRACEY POLLAN
  Met on *Family Ties*
- WARREN BEATTY and ANNETTE BENING
  Met while filming *Bugsy*
- SEAN PENN and ROBIN WRIGHT PENN
  Met on the set of *State of Grace*
- GOLDIE HAWN and KURT RUSSELL
  Started dating while filming *Swing Shift*
- PAUL NEWMAN and JOANNE WOODWARD
  Met when Newman starred and Woodward understudied in a production of *Picnic*
- SUSAN SARANDON and TIM ROBBINS
  Started dating while making *Bull Durham*
- Your favorite celebrity couple: _____

Don't Feel Left Out: You Too Can Be a Celebrity

Reality television shows have spawned a new crop of celebrities and, with their birth, a rash of new-celebrity couplings. The attention of the American public appears to have aphrodisiac qualities. Or maybe it's the diet of bugs and rice; *Survivor* seems to have particular success in pairing off the poor and beautiful. "Boston" Rob Mariano proposed to Amber Brkich in an especially dramatic fashion. Just moments before she was named the winner of *Survivor: All-Stars*, Mariano popped the question on bended knee in front of an international audience. CBS also paid for their on-air Bahamian wedding. And after flirting with contestant Julie Berry on *Survivor: Vanuatu*, host Jeff Probst got together with her after the cameras stopped rolling. "Once we started spending some time together, I didn't have any doubt," Probst told *People* magazine. And of course, who can forget the charming and gorgeous Trista and Ryan Sutter from *The Bachelorette* who live in Vail, Colorado, and occasionally hit the tabloids with announcements of the various stages of their engagement, marriage, and home life.

FAST FACT

If you always thought celebrities were more prone to self-involved behavior than the rest of us, you aren't wrong. A recent study of well-known people found them significantly more narcissistic than the average Joe. Noted one of the study's authors: "Female reality show contestants are off the chart." Moral of the story: Don't date a Survivor.

Not That You Should Always Emulate Celebs

Another thing about celebrity workplace romances: As you always suspected, these people do follow different rules, and you shouldn't always follow their example. Some of their behavior is relatively harmless—for them, anyway. Bill Gates and his future intended, Microsoft product manager Melinda French, were internally notorious for public displays of affection at employee picnics and other company events.

Other celebrity sins, however, are more serious than a few public kisses and hugs. Take adultery. For you and for us it can ruin not just a career, but a reputation. It goes without saying that beginning a romantic relationship with someone while already legally bound to another reflects badly on you—after all, most employers (and peers) value such traits as self-control and honesty.

For celebrities, however, chances are their careers will survive—even thrive—if they get a little on the side, no matter how dubious the circumstances. Movie studio honchos care if Brad Pitt can open a movie, not if he played fast and loose with his marriage vows when he made *Mr. and Mrs. Smith* with Angelina Jolie while still married to Jennifer Aniston. Ditto Bruce Springsteen, when he decided to leave his actress wife Julianne Phillips for E Street Band backup singer Patti Scialfa—someone, by the way, he had known for several years before romance bloomed. And Julia Roberts suffered not a whit (unless you count some embarrassing tabloid headlines) when she convinced cameraman Danny Moder, whom she met on the set of *The Mexican*, to leave his wife Vera and marry her instead. She even went so far as to wear a homemade T-shirt proclaiming "A Low Vera," a supposed reference to Vera's refusal to grant him a quickie divorce.

But if you collect a regular paycheck, from however exalted a position, taking marriage less than seriously with a work colleague is more serious stuff. In 1995 Boeing tossed out CEO Harry Stonecipher following the disclosure of his affair with a fellow executive, citing his "poor judgment." The *Harvard Business Review* canned head editor Suzy Wetlaufer when she began an affair with much-married then-G.E. Chairman Jack Welch after interviewing him for the magazine. Her bosses said it was a conflict of interest, but one wonders if the stench of nationwide bad publicity didn't affect their thinking—after all, they hadn't let Wetlaufer go when she was rumored to be liaising with an editorial assistant almost twenty years her junior. Then again, Wetlaufer couldn't have been feeling much pain; she and Welch were married a little over two years after she got the axe.

FAMOUS "DATES" IN OFFICE MATE HISTORY

1997 Staples Inc. president Martin Hanaka is forced to resign from his job after his secretary/paramour Cheryl Gordon called police, saying her boss had assaulted her in the course of a personal dispute. An argument, by the way, that took place in her apartment.

Bad Behavior in Service of the Public Good

We shouldn't have to tell you this, but even fame and power can't protect one from the consequences of illegal or unethical workplace behavior. Considering helping your sweetie to get a job he or she is completely unqualified for? Remember now-former New Jersey governor Jim McGreevey, who resigned from the governorship and embraced his identity as a "gay American" only after it was revealed he gave his lover a patronage job? How about World Bank head Paul Wolfowitz, who was forced out of the top post after it was revealed he engineered big pay raises for his then-girlfriend, a fellow Bank employee, even as he was leading an anti-corruption campaign?

And who can forget astronaut Lisa Nowak, trained to face the fear of death in space but somehow unprepared to face the heartbreaking loss of fellow astronaut William Oefelein. She drove from Texas to Florida in an adult diaper (the better to avoid the delays involved in taking bathroom breaks) to do bodily harm to her rival Colleen Shipman after using her key to Oefelein's apartment to spy on his computer and reading the steamy e-mails he had sent Shipman. Oefelein had sent Shipman love messages from his home computer, his office computer, and from the Space Shuttle. NASA's response to the imbroglio: "We don't track the personal lives of people who work for the agency."

No diapers, please. Whether you're a celebrity or an average Joe (or Joan), behaving like a baby is not the way to handle love.

takeaways from chapter 4

1. If you've always dreamed of being a celebrity, now at least you can act like one—by dating someone you meet through work.
2. If you're wondering why you should follow the guidelines we offer in this book, the celebrity-romance train wrecks you see in *People* magazine offer a good cautionary tale.

CHAPTER 5

You Think We're Not Talking about You, But We Are

You're not a celebrity, so you think we're not talking about you. Or you think we're not talking about you because you're not a twentysomething recent college graduate. You've concluded that that's who this book is written for, so you're convinced this book isn't for you. In fact, you didn't buy it. You've borrowed it from the twentysomething recent college graduate who lives down the hall in your apartment building. Or the twentysomething recent college graduate you gave birth to twentysomething years ago. Or the twentysomething recent college graduate you're dating in the wake of your recent divorce, even though you're fifty-three and suspect you should find someone more appropriate.

So let's address some of your ages, stages, and situations and correct your sad misimpression that *Office Mate* is not talking about you.

You're Not Looking to Get Married

True, we sometimes refer to the pot at the end of the workplace romance rainbow as being marriage, but if you notice, we do so only when we refer to studies that examine marriage as a consequence of dating a colleague. The two of us might have met our husbands at the office, but before they were our husbands they were our boyfriends. Seriously, who said every relationship worth having has to end in marriage? Not us. Whether you're looking for a life partner or a legal partner, we think you should look in the office, and we think you can do that without harming your career. Lisa and Tony are living proof of a long-term, happy office mating that shows no signs of progressing to the altar.

WATER COOLER CONFESSION

"don't rock the boat, baby"

"I had just changed jobs and two people told me to contact Tony, that he was the mover and shaker in my new organization and could help me fast-track my career. But I didn't. I was going through a divorce, though not many people knew about it, and I had three children to think about. I wasn't ready to put in the extra hours necessary to make a do-or-die project succeed. But we did eventually run into one another and it was immediately flirtatious. I was still wearing my wedding band and the first time we met he told me he wanted me to fix him up with someone like me! I told him I needed to get to know him better so I could find the right woman. Well, four months later I took the ring off and told him I had found someone just like myself: me! It's been almost ten years now and we have never gotten married. At first it was because I wasn't immediately divorced, and later I didn't want to upset my children, then there were work considerations . . . and now it just works the way it is. Why rock the boat when it is sailing just fine?" ◗

You're That Fifty-Three-Year-Old Divorcée in the First Paragraph

Or forty-three, or sixty-three. Divorced once, twice, three times—or perhaps widowed. *Office Mate* is perfect for you. In fact, the statistics show that sixty-three-year-olds are just as likely to find an office mate as twentysomethings: 38 percent of employees ages twenty-five to twenty-nine have had an office romance, while virtually the same number of workers fifty to sixty-four say they have had one.

Notice any significant difference between the number of younger people and the number of older people who have dated someone in the office? No, we didn't either.

Let's say you're a woman and you're headed back to the workplace because of a divorce or because your husband passed away. You haven't worked in a while, or maybe you worked damn hard but it wasn't the kind of work that paid the bills, which your husband's paycheck took care of. Maybe you worked part-time or at a nonprofit, or maybe you volunteered. The office is perhaps your best chance of meeting someone with whom you can start over.

FAST FACT

Careerbuilder.com surveyed workers to find out how many said they have had an office romance.

- Ages 25–29: 38 percent
- Ages 30–39: 47 percent
- Ages 40–49: 45 percent
- Ages 50–64: 36 percent

1861–1883 Following the death of her husband, Prince Albert, Queen Victoria becomes suspiciously close to Scottish servant John Brown. Gossip over the nature of their relationship is rampant, but it is never proven that the relationship was more than platonic. Historians still debate the possibility that the two secretly married.

If your long-term relationship has ended, you might find yourself in the market for a whole new social circle, not just a new romance. If you're divorced, your ex-husband might have custody of some of your friends. And if you're a widow, your social group might not know just what to do with you or your grief. Or they knew what to do to help when you were grieving, but now that you're ready to meet someone they might find themselves at a loss. Perhaps they think it's too soon. Or perhaps plenty of time has passed, but they feel disloyal to your husband's memory if they help you to find his successor. None of these concerns come into play at the office, as Linda's story demonstrates.

WATER COOLER CONFESSION

"the voice on the other end of the line"

"I was separated from my husband and our divorce was going on and on—it was very contentious. We fought over everything from child support to the furniture to who would pay for the kids' college educations. Romance was certainly the last thing on my mind and it's a good thing too, because in my small suburb my prospects for finding love weren't too terrific. I had to make a living and I hadn't worked since before my children were born, so I ended up taking a job as a secretary in a small office. My boss off-loaded a tremendous amount of his business dealings to me, so I did a lot more than take messages. One client was a man named Marty who had a whiskey voice but high, like a tenor, and he made me laugh. I started to look forward to his calls. We spoke regularly for weeks because there were so many details to work out in his business deal with my boss. We finally met on the day he signed the papers, and I was shocked to discover that he wasn't my type at all—he was shorter than I and heavy-set too, with a thick beard. But Marty had such a sparkle in his eyes and in that special voice that I was just as drawn to him as I had been on the phone. It turned out his marriage was also ending, and we were married six months after my divorce was final." ◢

Your Workplace Is a Romantic Wasteland

Funny you should mention it. Chapter 19 is all about exactly that. We would not be so clever if we wrote a dating book that could apply only to twentysomething women working in international conglomerates with offices in London, Paris, Rome, and Madrid.

Instead we've written a book about how every working woman can find love through her work. It doesn't matter if that work takes place at a desk at home, or a real estate agency filled with married ladies, or a beauty salon. Improbable as it may sound to meet a man through work under such circumstances, we'll tell you how. Chapter 19 awaits.

FAMOUS "DATES" IN OFFICE MATE HISTORY

1991 Anna Nicole Smith meets billionaire J. Howard Marshall while performing at Gigi's, a Houston strip club.

Which Means We Are Talking about You, All of You

If you're still not convinced that we're talking about you, kindly fill in the following sentence for yourself.

"I think *Office Mate* doesn't apply to me because

_____

_____

but I'm wrong. Almost anyone can meet a romantic partner through their work or workplace, finding a connection that is based on common interests and which will be more lasting than one found via the other typical ways of finding a mate."

Thank you.

Even if you have managed to avoid getting mixed up in a romance all these years on the job, there's little chance you haven't sensed the possibility. If you've never flirted with someone at the office, you're in a very small minority indeed.

FAST FACT

A comprehensive 2002 study of more than 31,000 men and women by *Elle* magazine and MSNBC found that 92 percent of subjects admitted to indulging in office flirtations. (Surveyors are still trying to figure out what was wrong with the other 8 percent.)

So, yes we are talking about you. Here are the facts: If you haven't met a steady by the time you enter the workforce, the chances are extremely high that you will—somehow, some day, some way—date someone you meet on the job.

takeaways from chapter 5

1. No matter who you are or what your age or situation, you can find love in the workplace. Trust us.
2. Marriage isn't necessarily the end-all and be-all of any romance, office or otherwise. We can help you look for a nice Saturday night date too.
3. You can work alone in a one-person office or among many in a same-sex office and still find love through your work.

CHAPTER 6

How to Indicate Interest—
Without Indicating Yourself Right Out of a Job

It could be love, it could be lust, but either way we've convinced you to follow your heart and get to know that attractive newbie in the marketing department just a little bit better. How do you move from office pal to office date without putting your job on the line, or risking utter humiliation and embarrassment?

We've got some ideas. But before we get to them, we want to make the point that unless your company has a specific ban on the activity, it is perfectly permissible to ask a fellow employee out on a date. It is not prima facie evidence of moral failure, a predatory nature, or, most important, sexual harassment (unless you are incapable of taking no for an answer).

We might also point out that romance and love are so individual and idiosyncratic that what works for one will not work for all. Our suggestions are by no means a formula. There are few absolutes when it comes to matters of the heart.

Last, we all know someone who broke the rules, as it were, and not only lived to tell about it but suffered not so much as a smidgeon of trouble. That doesn't mean you should take the following recommendations lightly. Why court disaster?

Recommendation No. 1: Take It Outside

We might call it workplace romance, but the less of it that goes on inside your actual workplace, the better. So when you're thinking of asking a coworker on a date, try hard—by which we mean really, really hard—to ask the question somewhere other than in your cubicle. Or the other person's cubicle. Or in a voicemail. Outside the building would be nice.

Think about it. This is someone you've been spending a lot of time with. You've felt a vibe. The vibe came from somewhere. It's likely you're not the only one who has been thinking about how to move your relationship to the next level. If you're comfortable enough with the guy to want to approach him, you should feel comfortable enough to do it someplace else.

This means waiting for your moment, which is fine by you because you're reading this book. Delayed gratification isn't a problem. So one night, when the office gang goes for drinks, ask your intended date if he would like a ride home. Or catch up with him as he is leaving the office for the day. You get the idea.

And if you truly cannot think of a way to make the approach outside the office, you might drop by your would-be office mate's workstation and suggest going for coffee. To a coffee place *outside* the office. Make certain no one overhears you; do it when the closest cubicle occupant is off to the bathroom or otherwise engaged. Do you want an audience to hear your proposition accepted, or worse, turned down? We didn't think so. Jonathan and Lily's story ends happily, but it almost didn't because of the public way in which he pursued her.

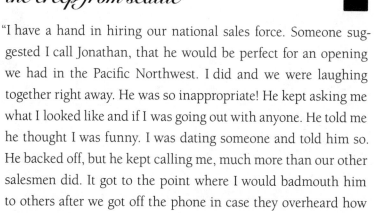

WATER COOLER CONFESSION

"the creep from seattle"

"I have a hand in hiring our national sales force. Someone suggested I call Jonathan, that he would be perfect for an opening we had in the Pacific Northwest. I did and we were laughing together right away. He was so inappropriate! He kept asking me what I looked like and if I was going out with anyone. He told me he thought I was funny. I was dating someone and told him so. He backed off, but he kept calling me, much more than our other salesmen did. It got to the point where I would badmouth him to others after we got off the phone in case they overheard how flirtatious we were getting. 'Jonathan's a creep,' I'd say. Finally, I broke up with my boyfriend and then had to go out to Seattle on business. I sent Jonathan a very casual note when I got to town, just saying it would be a good idea to finally meet in person. He wrote back immediately. 'You're here??' I picked up my cell phone and called him at once. We went out for a drink that night and he kissed me. I flew out again in two weeks—this time on my dime. We were engaged ten months to the day after we met. When I told my coworkers, they yelled out in unison, 'Jonathan's a creep!' It turned out I hadn't been fooling anyone." ◢

Recommendation No. 2: When All Else Fails, Try Happy Hour

We would be remiss if we failed to mention the opportunity to get to know your coworkers that most closely resembles the relaxed collegiate setting—at least when it comes to romance. That would be happy hour. Going out with the office gang after work is a low-pressure way to get to know someone. You usually have chaperones, and it's easy enough to separate off into a pair without attracting too much attention.

FAST FACT

According to Careerbuilder.com, 10 percent of office romances begin during happy hour.

Need we mention that many office mates credit alcohol's inhibition-reducing qualities as instrumental in moving their relationships forward? Need we further mention that other office mates say that imbibing caused them to make ghastly mistakes and errors of judgment? If you choose to drink, don't drive, as it were; starting an office romance in the company of a bunch of coworkers is tantamount to getting behind the wheel of a ton or two of serious machinery. Remember that going out with the gang, however relaxed or relaxing, is work-related. But there is no prohibition on a judicious mix of work and pleasure, as Isabel and Max found out.

WATER COOLER CONFESSION

"happy hour honeys"

"When I graduated from college I got a job with a bank as a business analyst. I met Max on my first day when I was taken around and introduced to everyone. Max says now that he even remembers what I was wearing—a red button-down shirt with black pants. He was a software developer, and even though we worked on the same floor we didn't get many opportunities to interact. But luckily almost all the new hires from the past few years went out in a group after work to get drinks several times a week. We even had a regular hangout. Soon Max and I were organizing the dates. I guess you could say in retrospect that we needed an excuse to spend time with each other. We would separate off, talk about our families and relationships of the past. This went on for months. Everyone knew about us but us. They kept saying, 'C'mon, you guys like each other.' But we remained just friends until one night just before the holidays. Once again a group of us went out after work. We wound up at a colleague's apartment. At some point we just went off by ourselves, like always. But this time it ended with us kissing! No one was surprised." ◢

Recommendation No. 3: Be Yourself, Really

We know, you're waiting for a caveat. Be yourself, but . . .

We understand. One of the biggest rules in *The Rules* is that a woman must not ask a man out on a date. Well, this is *Office Mate*, not *The Rules*. If you're the type of woman who generally makes the first move, go ahead (especially if he's not your boss or subordinate—we'll cover that in Chapter 12). The whole point of office romances is that they're based on who you really are, not the first impression you make. If you're a first-move type of gal, he probably knows that already. If he doesn't like it, you wouldn't want to date him anyway. You want someone who's happy to spend time with you—the real you, not your representative. But if, in your off-hours life, you would never ask a man out on a date, don't start doing it at the office. That just doesn't make sense.

Nonetheless, you might have to make things a mite easier for the guy you're interested in who, odds are, is interested in you too. He might be a little afraid here. He doesn't want to screw any number of things up—your career, his career, the comfort level you share as coworkers, the chemistry of your office gang—you name it. You'll have to find a way to show him that you're receptive to an advance. We don't really have to tell you how to do that, do we? Ask him to share a taxi ride home following those after-hours drinks we mentioned earlier. Go out for lunch, just the two of you.

Hey, any signal you send puts you ahead of the game, at least statistically. Halfpriceperfumes.co.uk, an online perfume seller that conducts surveys, queried people who had a crush on a colleague and discovered that three-quarters of them never let the other person know about their desires. The reason: fear of public humiliation or being forced to leave the company. But you don't have that fear, right? You've got guidelines to follow that will keep such dire consequences from happening.

Recommendation No. 4: Don't Ask Coworkers for an Assist

You simply cannot make your best office pal ask his best office pal if the cute guy in accounting likes you. You may not ask a colleague to perform a fixup. This is no time to devolve to your junior-high self. Yes, coworkers take on a valuable role in office romance—as we've said before, they can often spot a potential office mate and they tend to lobby for their pick. But it's one thing for them to lend a helping hand on their own initiative, and quite another for you to hit them up for an assist. Your colleagues are not romantic troubleshooters. You are in a workplace, collecting a paycheck, not sitting at a scratched-up, fake-wood desk studying for your geometry quiz. Act like it.

FAMOUS "DATES" IN OFFICE MATE HISTORY

1960 In the classic Billy Wilder film *The Apartment,* Jack Lemmon thinks he can get ahead at work by lending his pad to his bosses for adulterous get-togethers with underlings. Unfortunately, a superior is having an affair with the cute elevator operator Lemmon is falling for, played by Shirley MacLaine.

Recommendation No. 5: Don't Indicate Your Interest Via E-Mail

There are no caveats here, either. We *really, really* don't want you to use e-mail. And here are three reasons why:

- Because e-mail is the property of the company, and managers can (and do) read it whenever they damn well please.
- Because e-mail can be forwarded.
- Because e-mail, like a diamond, is forever.

If you can exercise any self-restraint whatsoever when it comes to office romance, this is where you should do it. Don't do *anything* via e-mail. Don't ask him out for dinner. Don't debate where to go for the dinner. Don't make a little joke about what might happen after dinner.

Why? How about this: According to the American Management Association, more than half of all companies retain and at least occasionally review employee e-mails. Moreover, slightly more than 25 percent of firms surveyed have fired at least one employee for inappropriate e-mail usage. Another 2 percent have let an employee go over similar abuses of instant messaging. And don't think picking up the phone is much safer: almost 20 percent of firms tape the calls of employees in certain job categories, with 15 percent reporting they tape or review voicemail.

That's right. There is no law stopping your bosses from reading your e-mail and IMs or listening in on your phone calls. So some of them do.

But hey—we know you're human and that it might well be unrealistic to expect that you will manage never to use e-mail to communicate with the one you want. We ourselves, along with many couples we interviewed for this book, have used e-mail to communicate with our loved ones on the cube farm.

We will go into this further in Chapter 10, but for now let us just say that if you are going to use e-mail or IM to communicate, don't do it until your relationship is established. You don't need to leave a trail of dating requests for any interested supervisor or tech to read. It's not about your workplace, it's about the nature of e-mail. It's messy. It makes a record. The record is easily transmittable. Moreover, there's no tone of voice to be heard, which is why e-mails are so easy to misinterpret. Why let yourself in for all that? Just say no. Conduct your personal business in person.

IM from PrivateJill   ✕

Not everyone works at a *Fortune* 500 company with professional spies reviewing every e-mail that goes in or out. I work at a small private school. We can't even afford a bus to send the kids on a field trip; I hardly think we're paying someone I've never heard of to see if I wrote to the principal to find out if he's free on Saturday night.

- -

Private, if your school has a computer network, it's got a network administrator. The function might be performed by an outside firm—that could be why you don't know about the guy. But somebody's running your system—keeping it going, running backups, the works. And that somebody can read your e-mails anytime he wants to, even if it's just to get his jollies. But let's say you're right—your workplace is so small that you don't have to worry. That doesn't mean you should gen- erate a record, especially a record that—as we mentioned above—your sexy principal can zip off to his friends after he tells you he'll be on a date with the school secretary on Saturday night instead.

E-mail is yet another *Office Mate* example of a case in which the old ways trump the new. Andie understood this intuitively.

WATER COOLER CONFESSION

"you can't forward paper"

"There was this dude in my office who was always flirting with me. But he was a junior staffer. I mean junior. He'd just gradu- ated from college and I'm going on thirtysomething. I knew I would have to make the first move, but I didn't want it to seem like harassment from a superior, nor did I want to embarrass myself—or leave myself open to future embarrassment. So I wrote him a note. By hand. I passed it to him in the hallway of our office at the end of the day. We went out for coffee the next night after work. As for the rest, you sure won't find out about it by following an electronic trail. There is none." ◢

Recommendation No. 6: No Games, Please, We're Adults

When you're trying to gauge someone's interest, don't be coy. Don't send an anonymous message and hope the person figures out it's from you. Don't hint. Be graceful. Be up-front. It's icky if you're not, as the following confession from Gina illustrates.

WATER COOLER CONFESSION

"no secret admirers wanted"

"On my birthday I received a card in my office mail saying 'Happy Birthday.' It was signed 'Your Secret Admirer.' Soon after roses and a jewelry box turned up signed the same way. I thought for sure it was my boyfriend, and I called him up to thank him. He denied all knowledge—in fact, he was angry. Finally, weeks later, my secret admirer revealed himself. He was a supervisor in my department. I was creeped out. He kept asking me out to coffee, refusing to take polite refusals. I finally told him I had a boyfriend. He stopped bugging me. It didn't impact my career any but it sure impacted my day-to-day comfort level in the office. In retrospect, I wish I had reported him to senior management."

More on this in Chapter 14, but until then, leave the Secret Admirer notes back in fourth grade where they belong. Actually, they didn't work so well back then, either.

Recommendation No. 7: Keep It Verbal

An easy way to end up on the wrong end of a sexual harassment suit is to show your interest rather than express it verbally.

You want to ask someone out for coffee? Fine, but do *ask*. Don't assume. You could be wrong. Remember, you're making room for rejection. How much room do you have if you've actually kissed an unwilling coworker? Or massaged their aching shoulders? Or rubbed up oh-so-subtly in the elevator? Ooo, not so much.

The odd office couple does result from an alcohol-lubricated grope on the dance floor at the office holiday party. Yes, we know some of them are in this book. Exception, not rule. Keep your hands to yourself. Remember what Mom used to say? Use your words.

Recommendation No. 8: Take No for an Answer

This one should be obvious, but if it were there'd be no such thing as sexual harassment law and a lot of attorneys would have to find another specialty. Not to mention the fact that you don't have to sexually harass someone to qualify as obnoxious. So what to do if the object of your affection says no?

> FAST FACT
>
> According to pollster Harris Interactive, 16 percent of men and 5 percent of women say their advances toward a colleague have been rejected.

Take it seriously—but lightly. Oh well. Anything else makes you seem like a stalker. That doesn't mean you can't stay friends with someone who has rejected your romantic advances. But it does mean no more queries unless the crush in question indicates a change of heart. In the meantime, résumé your previous relationship. Be chipper and professional. Be friends, or at least friendly. This holds whether you are the rejector or the rejectee. If you were rejected, the chances are your never-to-be inamorata does not want to be reminded of the incident any more than you do. Just, whatever you do, don't badmouth the person who has said no or whom you have turned down. This isn't junior high, and they don't have cooties. Sam recovered so gracefully from Stacy's initial rejection that they ended up together after all.

WATER COOLER CONFESSION

"a no that ended in a yes"

"My husband and I met at Apple nine years ago. We were working in the same group, and we had gone to Las Vegas for an industry convention. Late one night on the strip, Sam made a few drunken passes at me. His behavior aside, I thought he was cute—he had actually helped me out quite a bit getting the right programs on my computer and such—but I didn't want to get involved with someone from work. Too complicated. When we all got back from Las Vegas, Sam apologized for his behavior and I was impressed that he had the courage to admit and apologize, rather than just ignore. A few weeks later I took him out to dinner to thank him for all his help, but it wasn't a date. Finally he asked me out—gracefully this time—on a real date. And how. Sam said I had to wear a dress, and that we would have drinks at his house first, then off to dinner. I learned afterward that he had gone out to buy all the appropriate bar equipment and that his two best friends had helped him shop for just the right outfit (and I thought only girls did that). We kept things quiet for about five months, while we both worked there. We did such a good job keeping quiet that when we were at a trade show one of my friends wouldn't get lost because she was 'protecting' me from him. We've been married eight years now and just had our third kid. The group we were in has been reorg'ed a million times since, but we're still quite happy together." ◢

Recommendation No. 9: Don't Violate Sexual Harassment Law

Everyone cites the fear of sexual harassment when they discuss workplace relationships, but can you tell us what sexual harassment is? Write your answer below:

_____

Let's see how right you were. Sexual harassment is one of those terms all know but few can define.

FAMOUS "DATES" IN OFFICE MATE HISTORY

1991 Anita Hill comes forward to accuse future Supreme Court Justice Clarence Thomas of making inappropriate remarks and requests when the two worked together years earlier.

Sexual harassment originates in an amendment to Title VII of the Civil Rights Act of 1964, forbidding discrimination based on sex. Under federal law, there are two types of behavior that qualify as sexual harassment. The first is called *quid pro quo*. Usually involving a superior and a subordinate, the offending party must make a job or some aspect of the job dependent on receiving sexual favors. In other words, if someone offers you a promotion provided you will walk around their office naked, that's quid pro quo sexual harassment. If you refuse to walk around their office naked and suddenly find yourself the recipient of a negative evaluation or a pink slip, that's quid pro quo sexual harassment too.

But it's the other behavior that strikes fear into the hearts of many potential office mates. That's the so-called "hostile work environment" and it is by far the more common type of sexual harassment. It's when an employee engages in a consistent manner of inappropriate, sexually-based behavior that a colleague finds unwelcome or uncomfortable. A bunch of guys constantly talking porn in the presence of a lone female coworker can qualify. Constant unwelcome sexual banter meets the legal standard too. The key word here is "unwelcome." If you are considering flirting with a coworker whom you suspect won't be amused, stop considering.

FAST FACT

A survey by *Glamour* magazine and lawyers.com revealed that a quarter of employed adults believe they have experienced sexual harassment at work.

So where is the confusion? Well, ask ten people to define the word "inappropriate" and you get the gist of the problem. The Equal Employment Opportunity Commission—the federal authority better known as the EEOC, which is responsible for enforcing these laws—has said that Title VII does not make all sexual behavior in the workplace harassment. Not surprisingly, even judges have disagreed on what constitutes sexual harassment.

So can politely asking a coworker out for drinks be considered sexual harassment? It's pretty unlikely. After all, you are an adult who can say no or take no for an answer, right? Remember, the law says the requests have to be unwelcome. And you are unlikely to know that unless you ask.

But if you can't take a rejection, better to stay away from office dating. Repeated requests for romance in the face of rejection are no-nos. The law defines sexual harassment by the way the victim perceives it, not the way the harasser does. In other words, just because you thought it was a good idea to ask an unwilling person out on a date, say, a dozen times over the course of two weeks, doesn't put on you on the side of the angels. The infamous Anita Hill-Clarence Thomas imbroglio offers a lesson or two on how to avoid a charge of sexual harassment. Don't make repeated requests for dates after the first rejection. Don't boast about your sexual prowess or interest in pornography. And don't ask anyone you work with how a pubic hair got on your soda can.

Remember, though, this is all federal law. It's possible—in fact, it is likely—your firm will take a stricter view of things. It's their right. Again, we urge you to know your company's policies before indicating your romantic interest to a coworker.

What if you are a victim of sexual harassment or unwanted sexual attention in the workplace? First, tell the aggressor to cut it out. Begin to document incidents. Alert your supervisor. Tell Human Resources. This way you have a record if you want or need to pursue legal action.

One other thing worth noting: Sexual harassment does not only happen to women. Men can be victimized as well.

Now That You Know What Not to Do . . .

Let's review. You're not going to ask a coworker out while standing in your cubicle. You're not going to make use of e-mail.

office *mate*

You're not going to involve anyone else, and you're not going to do something you wouldn't do if the person you wanted to date didn't work at your firm. What *are* you going to do, then?

Do more of what you've been doing already. If you're attracted to someone in your office, you needn't do anything more than you are right now. You've got that pheromone thing going on. You're jazzed to come to work in the morning. You look your best, or at least, better than usual. You're probably even impressing the boss with your high-quality output (because, as we said earlier, you're not re-living junior high. You're doing better work than usual because of the buzz, not worse).

And once it's been established that you're going on your first official date, remember what you've learned so far. The fact that the two of you have so much to lose is a good thing. Go on a few more dates before you take it to the next level. Use the fear of jeopardizing your career as an excuse—it's true, isn't it? Then when you end up in bed, it's in the context of an established relationship, not a one-night stand. Not a bad thing at all.

takeaways from chapter 6

1. Take it outside.
2. Don't ask someone out while sitting at your desk. It's cheesy and unprofessional.
3. The days of asking a friend if somebody likes you are way over. And thank God for that.
4. E-mail is one of the Seven Deadly Sins of interoffice dating (or nine, if you've been counting). We take it back. It's all nine of the Seven Deadly Sins.
5. Don't ever set yourself up as a Secret Admirer.

CHAPTER 7

Let's Give Them Something to Talk About

Maybe you have scanned the field of eligible office mates and found no one who suits you. But like as not, other people have scouted on your behalf and they've found the perfect candidate. Whom should you thank for all this happy hunting? Your coworkers.

Say what?

This is the one traditional matchmaker function that your friendly Human Resources professional cannot perform, does not perform, and should not perform. That function is introducing you to The One. The members of the HR department certainly assemble a viable cast of characters, but they don't do the fixing-up— at least, not in a professional capacity. What they do on weekends is entirely up to them.

This is where your coworkers come in.

Normally coworkers are cast as the enemy in this equation: Before the romance begins, they're the competition—the other (sometimes) attractive people that a comely colleague might choose over you. Once the romance is under way, they're the source of gossip that could derail your career. They're the reason you supposedly keep your mouth shut.

Okay, we here at *Office Mate* agree that the office gang presents some problems of their own, which we will discuss at greater length later. But for now we need to point out their merits. Often, your coworkers know more than you think. And while that reality does have its downside, there is also a powerful upside. They add another layer of scrutiny, performing the final matchmaking steps after the HR department has stepped aside.

Remember, colleagues are the people in your village—the work village we identified at the beginning of this book. And like traditional neighbors, they will often identify your future office mate before you do. Like a nosybody watching from behind curtains to see what time you get home at night, they can sniff out a burgeoning relationship—even before the parties involved realize there is one. Other times, they will actively promote the possibility of a romantic relationship between two coworkers they believe to be a good fit, as with Janet and her handyman honey.

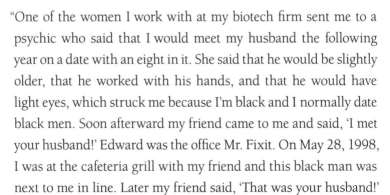

WATER COOLER CONFESSION

"psychic love connection"

"One of the women I work with at my biotech firm sent me to a psychic who said that I would meet my husband the following year on a date with an eight in it. She said that he would be slightly older, that he worked with his hands, and that he would have light eyes, which struck me because I'm black and I normally date black men. Soon afterward my friend came to me and said, 'I met your husband!' Edward was the office Mr. Fixit. On May 28, 1998, I was at the cafeteria grill with my friend and this black man was next to me in line. Later my friend said, 'That was your husband!'

After that day he started pulling work orders for my building. The day I got promoted he moved me into my office and I told him I owed him lunch. That's the first time I really looked hard at him, and he was everything the psychic had said he'd be, right down to the light eyes. He moved in by July and we were married two years later. The woman who had the office before I did had also met her husband there, so now there's a list of people who want to get in. They call it the Love Connection office." ◗

In short, your colleagues might very well be ahead of you. Rather than being shocked at the possibility that someone in their midst might be keeping an eye out for romance, colleagues are often the first to figure out there is—to quote folk rocker Bonnie Raitt—something to talk about.

FAST FACT

Surveyors say infidelity rises when participants hold jobs that require touching, talking, or being alone with others. The plus for you? This statistic may cause trouble for the married set, but it has obvious benefits for singletons.

Numerous subjects interviewed for this book report that rumors of a liaison frequently precede the first kiss. Annie from Chapter 3 returns to share how this worked in her case.

WATER COOLER CONFESSION

"smoke gets in your eyes"

"John and I met after we graduated from college and took the usual entry-level job at the same company. We were both miserable. We both had plans for ourselves that did not include doing everyone else's scut work. We became friendly because we were both smokers in those days. At first we would smoke in front of the building, but pretty soon we each figured out independently that if we stayed there we would be seen by our supervisors. We moved to the side of the building and soon we began going to lunch together too. Then 'accidentally' taking cigarette breaks at the same time. Everyone thought something more was going on, that we were dating. But we weren't. Even my boss began saying, 'John really likes you, why don't go out with him?' When we finally got together romantically, it could not have been more banal. It was at the firm's Christmas party. We both got really drunk and ended up going back to his apartment. As for my boss, he was so approving that after we finally debuted in public as a couple, we double-dated with him and his wife!" ◐

What is it they're picking up on that you're not? Perhaps it would be helpful if we broke it down a little.

How Your Coworkers Identify a Dark-Horse Potential Office Mate

- They see you making a habit of eating lunch with a colleague you don't consider yourself attracted to.
- They watch you linger after hours to leave the office together, maybe share the walk home or grab a drink.
- They spot you hanging around someone's cubicle for no obvious reason.
- They observe the same someone hanging around your cubicle for no obvious reason.
- They notice that you always ask said someone for advice even though there are plenty of other coworkers around with the same expertise.

- Or, in a twist, they might feel that your sparring with a colleague whom you butt heads with indicates a spark rather than a rivalry.

Once again, take a hint from Bonnie Raitt: If you're looking at each other a little too intently or forever finding a seat close by, you might not think anything of these signs. But your nosy associates most certainly will.

IM from GetReal   ✖

I find what you're saying offensive. Not every friendship between male and female colleagues is romantic in nature. Sometimes two people just get along well. Insinuating that such relations always have a sexual component doesn't do wonders for women in the workplace. You are making us seem like a bunch of bimbos killing time on the job while we wait to acquire the office equivalent of an MRS degree. I don't want to live in a world where I can't have a male mentor, or a friendship with a male colleague, without everyone thinking something romantic is going on.

- -

Real, we have two words for you. Harry. Sally. If you have a friendship with someone of the opposite sex, there will always be people (of the Harry stripe) who will assume there is something between you, even if that's not remotely the case. That's reality. What is also reality is that if your work relationship does have that component, it doesn't mean you need to or want to act on it. We're only suggesting you consider the possibility if you are looking for love. You're not, so don't. You have our blessing.

Trust Your Colleagues' Judgment

If you are in the market for a romantic relationship, you might want to consider that your colleagues are valuable sources of information. They frequently note minor character traits—both good and ill—that you might overlook. And you ought to have some respect for their opinion, which we can guarantee they will share with you whether you want to hear it or not.

Why should you respect their opinion? Because they're a tough crowd. Like villagers dependent on each other for food, sustenance, and entertainment, modern coworkers also need one another to thrive. And if someone routinely comes to work late, turns in sloppy or unacceptable work, is a terrible gossip, or is otherwise unreliable, their associates are often the first to know. As a result, professional colleagues are in possession of some vital information about your potential crush's character that would not be obvious if you met, say, in a bar or online.

Ways in Which the Office Gang Is an Even Tougher Audience Than HR

- Before too long, the new hire has been taken out for drinks and sized up.
- Soon he's made a friend who then takes his measure as a person.
- When the first work crisis hits, everybody watches to see what he's made of.
- If he makes other people look bad or makes their work harder, they have no problem reporting on him with abandon, both to you and to his superiors.
- If he wins the day they start looking out for him and helping him to succeed—both in and out of the office.

What the office gang concludes about a could-be office mate of yours after they've completed their vetting process can prevent you from making a mistake, whether the guy's a new hire or celebrating several years with the same firm. Considering the stakes involved in making romantic mistakes at your workplace, that's not nothing.

FAMOUS "DATES" IN OFFICE MATE HISTORY

1987 In the movie *Broadcast News*, Albert Brooks keeps Holly Hunter's hyperethical news producer from making the mistake of acting on her unlikely attraction to William Hurt's slimy anchorman by telling her that he worked up tears for a newspiece cutaway shot to heighten ratings.

What's more, the office gang can function as the actual matchmakers. A number of successful couples interviewed for this book reported that colleagues shoved them into coupledom— some pushing them to consider someone they would never have thought about, others elbowing them from flirtation to dating. Remember Meredith Vieira? She and her future husband managed to flirt all on their own, but it took the intercession of a work colleague—one who sent them out to dinner together—to make them get it together and actually date. Wendy's boss really went above and beyond.

WATER COOLER CONFESSION

"i like your vibe"

"I took a summer job as an office manager in a physical therapy practice to see if the career would suit me. On my first day of work, my new boss kept mentioning a client, Jake, due to come in later that day. I thought it was a bit odd and I figured she must be dating him or something. When Jake finally arrived, I chatted with him for a bit and then got on with my work. Later that day my boss asked me to go with her to a meditation class. Again, there was Jake. We chatted longer this time—and ended up going out to dinner. The next day Jake turned up at the office at closing time. We again all went to a yoga class and, again, to dinner. We moved in together within six weeks of meeting and eventually married. When I asked her after the fact, my boss simply said she 'had a feeling based on our energy fields.' Whatever, it worked. What's more, I'm now a physical therapist too!" ◐

One caveat about the above Water Cooler Confession: Don't try this at home. We weren't thinking that dozens of you are going to write to us after reading Wendy's story to tell us that a colleague sized up your energy field and found you a life partner. But we do think that your colleagues are a fabulous asset to your possibly happy and successful romantic future, and you should take advantage.

Does that mean they're always right? Hardly. Does that mean you should spend your days gossiping with your office friends about which colleague you should hit on? Not so much. So here are some specifics.

Listen to a colleague's suggestion of a potential office mate if . . .

- You value that colleague's judgment in other matters, especially everyday business doings.

- You're surprised that colleague would say something (in other words, this isn't someone who's trying to make trouble).
- The colleague knows both of you well enough to make an educated guess about whether you're compatible.
- The colleague knows the person so well that they can offer a considered recommendation.

Disregard a colleague's suggestion of a potential office mate if . . .

- They pride themselves on their matchmaking abilities (when the office gang spots a potential romance, it's based on the evidence, not a hobby).
- The office mate they identify is inappropriate—married, thrice-divorced, a hound, etc.
- You had a moment of weakness and asked a colleague which coworker you should ask out. The idea is that the office gang *comes to you* to propose a dark horse—you don't solicit the information.

When the suggestion is made, listen and then don't indulge in further speculation with the party who made it. In no time, what you say will be whispered into the wrong ear and you'll get into that seventh-grade does-he-like-me game. Not appetizing.

But let's say their suggestion proves to be brilliant. How much do you owe the person (or gang) who matched you and your office mate? Do you owe them, for example, information?

No. What you owe them is courtesy and consideration. That means you keep things to yourself and disclose as necessary.

Respond to rumors with a gentle demurral that bores the gang into dropping the subject. But while you are guarding your privacy, be as polite and sweet with them as possible. At some point you can most likely confirm their suspicions, and when you do, give thanks.

takeaways from chapter 7

1. Your colleagues may see things in your behavior that you can't.
2. You might consider that they can be better judges of romantic potential than you are.
3. If you are spending an unnecessary amount of time with a fellow worker, you might want to ask yourself why.
4. Dating at the workplace does not have to set back the feminist movement. In fact, it better not. As working mothers, we want no part of turning back the clocks, feminist or otherwise.

CHAPTER 8

What about the "Office Spouse"?

To office spouse or not to office spouse? That is the question.

So what is an office husband or wife? An office wife is a man's right-hand-woman at work, someone who is his professional and possibly personal confidante, who reads his mind and laughs at his jokes and goes out to dinner with him on business trips and does just about everything but sleep with him. And an office husband serves the same function to a female employee, regardless of whether either one has a legal spouse at home.

In other words, they are best friends, something everybody could use in the workplace. And there is an added benefit: Many management consultants say that the men and women in these relationships tend to be less competitive with one another than even the best same-sex workplace pals. As a result, each can modulate the other's moods and act as a buffer when things are not going well in a way that even a more-conventional best friend cannot.

The concept of the office spouse has gone public and high-profile like never before. In 2004, political journalist Timothy Noah argued that President George W. Bush was the first president in modern history to have a work wife in addition to his real wife, Laura. In fact, Noah wrote, Bush had at least two such relationships in the White House.

FAST FACT

According to our friends at The Vault, almost one-third of employees has an office "husband" or "wife."

The first was with Karen Hughes, a communications counselor and general advisor. When she decided to return to Texas, Bush appeared to mourn. Shortly thereafter, he re-"married"— with Secretary of State Condoleeza Rice. And just to prove how controversial this sort of arrangement can be, the Bush-Rice "marriage" was the staple of tabloid headlines thereafter. The gossip, no doubt, was fueled by the behavior of at least one of the participants. Rice herself referred to Bush in public at least once as her "hus-" before catching and correcting herself.

But is it appropriate to have such an intense relationship with a colleague of the opposite sex? Are the benefits of these fabled alliances all they are cracked up to be? And just how easy is it to cross the line from faux romance into the real thing?

The Office Spouse: Pros

Fans of the office spouse relationship point to the bond of common experience: work.

"My wife, that is my real wife, doesn't want to hear about the office that much," says Jay, a film executive. "She can't hear almost the same story about the same stupid boss every day. But my other wife—my office wife—she can hear it and add a few stories of her own."

And Jan, who left her job at an advertising firm when her son was born, still talks by phone to her office husband at least once a week. "He needs to vent," she shrugged.

Office spouses sometimes do turn into the real thing, but it can be a painful process, as the following confession from Kris illustrates.

WATER COOLER CONFESSION

"what an agoreable couple"

"Holly and I were both working in Washington, D.C., at the Office of Scheduling and Advance. We coordinated the schedules of Vice President Al Gore and his wife. The hours were ridiculous, so we spent a lot of time together. We became close friends and it was clear there was something there, but at the time I was seriously dating someone else in our sphere. My girlfriend and I had a lot of fun, but I realized that our core beliefs were different once I started spending more time with Holly. For close to two years nothing happened, until one day Holly and I were standing in the street and she asked, 'When are we going to stop denying this attraction for each other?' I broke up with my girlfriend. I asked Holly to keep the relationship quiet for two years for fear of alienating my ex. Eventually I decided to move back to California where we're both from, and Holly agreed to move with me. I was amazed she stuck by me through all this. I asked her to marry me right before the move, in the bell tower near the Iwo Jima Memorial." ◗

The Office Spouse: Cons

For office spouses who remain platonic, complications can arise that eerily echo the pitfalls of traditional romantic relationships. The twosome can become so close that they shut out others—in this case, colleagues. That's not so good for the career, since colleagues are your eyes, ears, and compatriots in the office. Even if platonic office couples don't actually shut out their coworkers, the couple may manage to alienate them by inspiring jealousy. Coworkers have any number of things to be jealous of when it comes to office spouses. There's the strength-in-numbers aspect of the relationship, to start with, not to mention the possible advantages of information passed between the pair that might enhance both their careers while letting the office gang drag along behind. And of course there's the perception that office spouses are indeed engaging in a romantic relationship, however vociferously they may protest to the contrary.

IM from HormoneGal ✕

You're talking about office spouses who remain platonic as if that's even possible. Don't we all agree by now that men and women can't just be friends? Isn't there always a buzz between them, especially between a man and woman who are so drawn to each other as to form a bond like this at work?

- -

We're not going to fight with the oft-cited theory that when a man and a woman are friends there's always a little something of a buzz between them. But that doesn't mean it's the right kind of buzz to spark or sustain a romantic relationship.

> Perhaps we could all agree that there can be the
> kind of buzz between a man and a woman whose
> intellects and professional interests jibe enough
> to click at work but not outside of it? Not to
> mention the fact that, buzz or no buzz, office
> spouses are adults and generally act like it.

Moreover, having an office spouse can occasionally cause serious trouble in the lives of married or otherwise-committed folks. According to the late Shirley Glass, a noted infidelity researcher, acquiring a close office companion of the opposite sex can be the first step toward having an affair. In her book, *Not "Just Friends": Rebuilding Trust and Recovering Your Sanity after Infidelity,* Glass writes that one sign of trouble is when a person confides more in their office spouse than in the legal spouse waiting at home. "In many cases, the transition from friendship to affair is barely perceptible—to both participants and observers," she writes, adding a sage bit of wisdom from her son, *This American Life*'s Ira Glass: "You know you're in trouble when the word 'just' appears before the word 'friends.'"

We would point out that in this case you should break up with your office spouse, not your real spouse, but you don't have a real spouse. You're looking for one. So instead we'll go on to explain that another difficulty is that like real couples, platonic partners at the office can get on each other's nerves. They can bicker and squabble, especially when real-couple problems plague them, such as when one spouse takes it upon himself to speak for the other to outsiders, or when one spouse takes the other for granted, expecting favors rather than being graciously surprised by them. Then a couple can go through all the Don'ts of true office mates, from the big fight to the urge to divide the office gang into His and Hers. (In which case, follow the guidelines that appear in the second half of this book for enduring these trials with minimal fallout.)

This is one of the genuine Cons of the office spouse—if and when the big fight takes place, it seems to do so with all the attendant ire of a marital breakup rather than with the quieter crack between same-sex friends who realize that there wasn't as much binding them together as they originally thought.

Many office spouse relationships come to a natural end, with both participants slowly distancing themselves from the partnership. Sometimes, alas, one partner will want to move on to greener pastures—at least office–spouse-wise—when the other does not. These office spouse endings, with no big fight and no mutual agreement that this arrangement is no longer working, can sometimes end in hurt feelings. Bob, an Internet denizen, recalls waiting in vain for his office wife to realize he would like to take their relationship to the next level. She didn't. "Never again," he says. "I didn't go on a date for a year because of her."

FAMOUS "DATES" IN OFFICE MATE HISTORY

2006 Famed marketing wunderkind Julie Roehm is fired from a top job at Wal-Mart after rumors of a "personal" relationship with a male subordinate sweep the company, which bans such connections. Roehm and junior employee Sean Womack (both married to others) deny all wrongdoing but both find themselves job-hunting, with the added handicap of their rumored affair splashed across the pages of national newspapers.

Finally, there are those who consider the relationship to be thankless, particularly when the office couple in question have unequal roles. An office wife who is a secretary to an office husband who is a CEO can feel used, particularly when she is passed over for promotions she has earned because her boss finds he can't live without her.

You don't need to fall into these traps. Here's how:

Six Rules for the Office Spouse

1. Don't do anything you wouldn't do to your best and oldest girlfriend. Planning to kiss your best friend on the lips soon? Toss her over the copier? We didn't think so. Don't do it to your office spouse either.

2. Don't get caught in compromising positions. Doors should remain open and intentions out in the open. People are likely to gossip about your alliance no matter how you behave. You don't need to encourage them.

3. Resist developing a crush on your office husband. It's unlikely to end well. Especially if he has a legal spouse.

4. Infidelity, in this case, is okay (platonic infidelity, that is). Many workplace "spouses" are situation-specific. Get a new job or a new boss? Often a new workplace mate will soon follow.

5. Make sure your office spouse's wife knows you. Nothing breeds jealously and suspicion like a lack of actual knowledge. One husband and wife team we interviewed—each of whom has a platonic office spouse—makes sure to meet for lunch as a foursome a few times a year.

6. If his real-life partner or your real-life partner objects, so long office spouse.

The only way to violate that last one is to forget who your real partner is. And if you're inclined to forget that, do something about it. We hear there are other fish in the sea. Have an idea where we think you should go fishing?

---

takeaways from chapter 8

1. Mistakenly calling your office spouse your "hus-" is not clever at all.
2. Doing so within hearing of your real "hus-" could actually land you in "div-" court.
3. As many advantages as you may have at work when you've got an office spouse, it's a relationship that requires a double dose of vigilance to keep from going terribly awry.
4. But if you're having romantic thoughts about your office husband and he happens to be available, consider acting on them. If he isn't, a "div-" of the office variety might be in order.

PART 2

office mate etiquette: managing your workplace romance

CHAPTER 9

So You're in Love: Dos

Congratulations! You or your pals at work have found you the perfect office mate, and your first date was successful, not to mention your second. But wait, where are you going? Did you think we were all done?

Don't shut the book; we're just getting started. After all, if you want to keep both your office mate and your job, you'll need to know the finer points of workplace romance etiquette. Remember, you are conducting a romance in the twenty-first-century village. You've read enough of this book by now to know what that means. Many eyes are watching you. Sure, they might be peeping over cubicles or around cash registers instead of out cottage windows and over plows, but the effect is the same. These modern-day villagers will be just as happy as their predecessors to gossip about the ups and downs of your relationship—if you provide them with juicy tidbits. Many of them will wish you well but, just like their feudal counterparts, there are a few who don't have your best interests at heart.

IM from ILoveMyJobAndMyJobLovesMe ✕

Why so much doom and gloom? I love my coworkers and my job, and they love me right back.

- -

Well, maybe not all of them do. Maybe one wishes you would take a misstep so that you might not be such tough competition for the next promotion. So if you were to fight in the office, have sex on your boss's desk, exchange X-rated e-mails, or give your colleagues daily weather reports on your relationships, your rival might make hay. Why make it so easy?

But in a concession to Lover above, we'll be positive. We'll start with the Dos of office romance, not the Don'ts. We won't even let the Don'ts infect the Dos; we gave them their own chapter.

Do make sure you have more than the workplace in common.

Like soldiers in wartime, coworkers who have mutual interests beyond the workplace often become best friends (and more). This phenomenon is so well-documented that sociologists have a term for it: propinquity.

FAST FACT

"Propinquity" was first articulated by a group of sociologists in the 1950s studying apartment-building life. They determined immediate neighbors were most likely to be friends. Least likely: those living on separate floors. Intriguingly, those living in spots where they would interact with all residents (near stairs and mailboxes) enjoyed friendships with people throughout the building.

But time may prove that what felt like a love connection was really just an illusion created by the job. Office marriages that end in divorce often follow this trajectory. You and your office honey don't have to join them. There are ways to figure out whether you're the real thing or merely a product of battle fatigue. For example, do you spend an awful lot of time talking about that amazing project you were both assigned? Are all your mutual friends people from the office?

The trick is to distinguish whether the two of you have so much in common as people, or whether the thing you both have in common is your company. It's kind of like the dance that people who meet in a bar have to perform. Did they really click as people, or were they just sexually attracted to each other?

But you have an advantage. The fact that you met in the office means you probably knew your office mate quite well before you went on an official date. What you have to navigate carefully is the transition from being a platonic unit inside the office to being a romantic unit outside the office. Take note of what you're doing together during your off-hours and whom you see. Are you building the beginnings of a life together that is composed of elements found outside the office—his friends, your friends, his family, your family, his passion for hiking and yours for bicycling, and so on? It's easy to let your mutual irritation with your strident boss be the main topic of conversation. Don't give in.

Do keep your membership in the office gang alive after you've started dating someone (whether that person is a member of the gang or not).

This is one of the easiest mistakes to make, one of the least necessary to make, and one of the most important to avoid making.

You're dating someone at work—now is not the time to alienate your other coworkers. They are your eyes and ears. They might even have helped you find your office mate in the first place. You owe them. But if you don't watch out they could become your enemies. Why put yourself in the position of having to worry about them?

Don't change your behavior around the office gang just because you're in a relationship. If you used to go drinking with them on Friday night, go drinking with them on Friday night (and if you used to do it without your office mate, don't always bring him along). If you used to play in a softball league, don't leave your team with an empty bat. In other words, don't do that teenage-girl thing. Don't dump your friends just because some guy called. Nobody likes it. Neither will your office mate, because the other thing nobody likes is when someone they just started dating drops all their commitments in hopes of spending every spare moment together. How dull.

Do choose restaurants and after-hours venues where you're not likely to bump into your colleagues.

If you live in a small town with only three eateries, obviously you can ignore this one. You're merely one half of a couple trying to date with a tiny measure of privacy, you're certainly not 007. It's just that it's worth the effort to use a bit of discipline to keep private things private and to leave the office at the office, so why hang out where you're likely to be scrutinized (and later, gossiped about)? You may as well avoid it, provided it's avoidable.

Do find out what you're like as a couple around other couples. Meaning, regular couples. Not other office couples.

Listen, we acknowledge that working with someone you date can be weird. All that secrecy can be damaging, or it can have the opposite effect and make your relationship seem hotter than it really is. The constraints around you can lend themselves to drama. So outside the workplace you need to be as normal as possible. It's vital, in fact, if either or both of you have long-term designs. You need to double-date with couples from your social circle, go away for a weekend alone, take each other to meet your families, all that everyday stuff. Defuse the 007 aspect. Build up an identity as a couple that is independent of the company where you met. Make sure there is a You, as opposed to a You-as-a-Subset-of-Your-Corporate-Parent. You're not kids, and your company is not your daddy. Don't let your relationship be marginalized by that dynamic.

Do be clear about what you're doing and where it's going.

This is another case in which office romances depart radically from relationships formed on the spot by people who have just met for the first time. Yes, you could say there's more at stake in an office relationship (your career, for one thing) than in a relationship that started in a bar or on the Internet, but there's a lot at stake no matter how you meet. This is your heart, after all. You're not looking to get it broken. But let's be frank: an office relationship is one between two people who already know each other pretty well as acquaintances and who would like to keep their careers going just as well as they were before the relationship started. So you need to have a different discourse early on than the couple at the bar, who have to build whatever will be between them completely from scratch.

We're not saying that you should sit across from your office mate while eating your first romantic dinner and declare that you're on the hunt for a husband. Yikes. But early on, perhaps even *before* you're having that first romantic dinner, make it clear that you're not going to cross that line for a one-nighter. Any number of sentences will take care of this issue without making you look like a crazed spouse-seeker. We can think of three right off the bat:

- "I wouldn't get involved with someone at the office unless I thought the person was worth the risk to my career."
- "I'm worried that if things don't work out between us I'll lose our friendship."
- "I think that when people get involved at the office one of them eventually has to leave, and I can't imagine either of us doing that."

Note that we mean for you to make a small effort to make sure you're not taking unnecessary chances for the wrong person. Some people on the west coast seem to have taken this to rather an extreme. Witness a law firm in San Francisco that has a unique specialty: drafting love agreements for dating coworkers. Both partners sign that the relationship is consensual. It's called "the love contract."

Clarification: no need to take it that far.

Clarification, part two: these contracts have not been tested in court, so who's to know how much protection they offer?

1998 San Francisco employment and labor relations law firm Littler Mendelson pioneers the love contract—called a "consensual relationship agreement"—in the wake of the Bill Clinton–Monica Lewinsky scandal. Partners estimate they have drafted at least 1,000 of the fabled agreements since then.

If you have to tell someone about your relationship, do tell your boss first.

We're not saying you have to tell your boss. In many circumstances you don't. If the two of you work for the same company but not for each other, or not in the same department, don't worry about it. Especially if the information you have as a result of your position doesn't compromise or give an undue leg up to your office mate in another department (and vice versa). But there are obvious times when you have to come clean. When one of you supervises the other (in which case, read Chapter 12 for details on how to handle this whole messy enchilada). When you're competing for a promotion or an assignment. When one of you is in a position to give the other vital information he or she wouldn't otherwise have. Or when one of you needs help moving back across the country, as in Leslie's unusually epic Office Mate story.

WATER COOLER CONFESSION

"bad timing?"

"I was from the east coast but I worked at a large bank in California. After five years I decided it was time to go back home, so my office pal Connie and I decided to pool our stuff and have a joint garage sale to cut down on the number of things I'd have to move. On the day of the garage sale, a guy named Bill from Connie's department came to drop off some paperwork. I'd gone with her to several of her department's events, so it's amazing I'd never met Bill before. He and I got to talking and we hit it off, so when it was time to get dinner we asked Bill to join us. Connie said, 'You have to date him.' And I said, 'I'm not going to date this guy. I'm moving across the country in six weeks!' But the very next day Bill and I went out to dinner, and the night after that he cooked dinner for me, and as I watched him chop the vegetables for pasta primavera I felt like I had known him for ten years. I felt so comfortable and so at home with this person, and I'd never had that experience with a man before. So I left California, but I didn't stay away too long because Bill and I flew back and forth to see each other and spoke on the phone so much that one month's bill was $300. After six months I asked the bank to give me a job back at the branch, and they did. We were married five years later." ◗

In circumstances when your romance compromises the integrity of your jobs, don't let your boss be the last to know. Wait, certainly, until you know there's something substantial and long-term developing between the two of you. If you've been following our guidelines, you should be able to do this without becoming the talk of the office. And that's good, because when you're the talk of the office your options for letting the right people in on it at the right time and in the right order are taken away from you.

But we trust you. We have faith that your boss hasn't already heard about your romance from someone else. If you work for the same boss, that means one of you should go to her—never both of you together, or it will feel like you turned yourselves in to the principal, and never via e-mail—and tell her that you are dating seriously and you don't want to put her in a difficult position later by not giving her the heads-up. Tell her that if she feels she needs to address the situation so that neither of you is in a position that's compromising to the company, you'd like to work with her on a solution. And do so in a matter-of-fact, non-007-type way. No drama. You're just doing the responsible thing and enlisting her in your effort. You're not selling state secrets here.

Do discuss the worst-case scenario.

Yes, we know this subject is a downer. Who wants to think about the end of the affair when you are at its beginning? Yet the beginning is the best time to discuss how you will handle things if one of you, one day in the future, no longer sees a point to your strategic alliance.

Office mating, however effective for finding true love, puts certain constraints on relationships that develop and take place within its environs. When you break off, say, an Internet relationship, it doesn't really affect your day-to-day life. After all, you never would have met if it weren't for the Internet and you are unlikely to see much—if anything—of each other now. If you were to have a public confrontation it would be embarrassing but is unlikely to do your life or career any real harm. It goes without saying that this is not true of workplace romance.

When love ends with an office mate, however, you are likely to still see each other. Even if you are not in the same department.

Or on the same floor. There is the elevator bank. And the company cafeteria. And the Christmas party.

As a result, many business management experts urge office lovebirds to review how they will handle the end when they are just starting out. You know, when you have stars in your eyes. When you cannot imagine anything, ever, going wrong. This way, the conversation remains hypothetical. And rational. It does not get defensive. It does not degenerate into a "state of the relationship" session. What it does is give you an idea of how you will go forward if you ever break up.

Sample Topics to Discuss

- Whether and how we will tell others in the office about the end of our romance.
- What we can and can't divulge to fellow employees about our relationship or each other's personal histories/habits.
- The absolute prohibition against recriminations in the office, no matter how tempting.
- Write your own ground rules here:

_____

_____

_____

_____

_____

_____

_____   _____

Sign your name   *He signs his name*

Now, if this conversation does become contentious, consider the prenup effect. The necessity of signing a prenup before taking their wedding vows puts some women in a situation where they'll get a lot of valuable information about this hubby-to-be of theirs. Either the discussions surrounding the prenup are going to confirm their choice or wave a bunch of red flags. Same with the prebreakup conversation. Whatever goes on between you, take note. You could save yourself a lot of time and grief.

A parting thought: When people disparage the very notion of office romance, it is the post-split scenario that they often cite. But we feel compelled to point out that plenty of other methods of meeting someone involve contact that is likely to persist after a breakup. If you meet in college and break up there are myriad painful points of contact. If you meet through friends or family it's the same. Even breaking up with someone you met via the Internet offers a number of self-flagellating postbreakup possibilities that include checking your ex's profile for updates on his conquests. Just about everyone who sees their ex after the relationship ends lives to tell the tale. So will you. And your career will continue to thrive too.

Do be proud, not loud.

This entire book may strike you as rather defensive, but that's not really our point of view. As you know, we believe office romance has gotten a bad rap. So what do you have to be defensive about? You found love in a place where you spend most of your daylight hours consorting with a lot of smart, compatible people. Why *wouldn't* you have found a partner thus? Just because you keep things to yourself doesn't mean you're ashamed. It's just strategic, diplomatic, mature. It's not a sign that you think you're doing something wrong. We certainly don't think you're doing something wrong, and as long as you examine your situation from your company's perspective and keep your liaison on the right side of company policy, your company doesn't think you're doing something wrong either. You're not loud, but you still get to be proud.

takeaways from chapter 9

1. Be afraid of the possibility that all you really have in common is your toxic workplace or your treacherous boss. Be very afraid.

2. By its nature, the way you met your office mate has some dramatic aspects. Make your relationship the opposite.

3. Contemplating involvement with a coworker is the only dating situation in which it's kosher to suss out how serious the other person is about you early on. Your mother would approve.

4. The downside of getting the chance to find out how serious he is early on is that you also have to discuss what to do if the relationship ends. You live by the sword, you die by the sword.

CHAPTER 10

So You're in Love: Don'ts

Here they are, the Don'ts of office romance, off in their own chapter where they won't do any harm to the nice, positive Dos. But, sadly, we must express them, much though it causes us nice, positive *Office Mate* promoters some pain. Such is life.

Don't conduct any part of your office romance in the office.

Perhaps you're surprised to read the above. Here we are writing a whole book about the advantages of office romance and we don't want you actually to *have* an office romance? So let's be clear. We think you should be open to the idea of *meeting* your significant other in the office. We hope we've made a solid case for the meeting part. Where we depart from your assumptions is in saying that you shouldn't *romance* your office mate in the office. The office is for work. You should work at the office.

You should strive to have a love life on your own time, as Ruth and Paul did.

WATER COOLER CONFESSION

"our company was never the wiser"

"I got married very young, and things were rocky. Then I met Paul while working for a large manufacturing company. We were in different departments, but right after I was hired, during my tour of the office, I saw him out of the corner of my eye. He saw me too, and made up some budget issue as an excuse to come and meet me. Once in a while we'd go to lunch, nothing else, until I left my husband. Paul and I never gave the least indication to anyone we worked with that we were seeing each other; they didn't even know I had separated from my husband. Paul would sit in his little car in front of my apartment and wait for me to get home from school at 10:30 every night. I never told anybody at the company about Paul. Paul left for a better opportunity a few months later and went to work somewhere else. Then I left for another company maybe six months after that. We got married two years after first meeting, and we've been married for twenty-five years." ◗

Don't have an argument in the office.

Ever. No matter how much your office mate done you wrong. We don't care if you just discovered your beloved was really the second coming of Casanova. We don't care if you discovered he blew off dinner with you to do his ex-girlfriend's laundry. You can't bring it into the office. Argue at home. Call him at night to chew his head off. But don't go after each other at work. Don't even exchange a dirty look.

We hardly need explain why. You will look unprofessional. You will look immature. You will provide your coworkers with hours of entertainment at your expense. And since not everyone in the office is your friend, there's at least one person who will be delighted to use any negative information about you to his or her own benefit. Don't provide ammunition.

Moreover, you and your office mate are not the only two people who might suffer the consequences—your arguing can victimize others as well. To show how, we're changing our usual water cooler confession here. Instead of a couple telling about their fights in the office, we'll hear from Larry, the poor, unwilling audience of such a twosome.

WATER COOLER CONFESSION

"i told you so"

"I had just started a new technology job and when I got to my pod I realized I was seated with a married couple. I knew there were going to be problems within twenty-four hours. In one of their conversations the husband was stumped because a customer was being difficult and he wasn't sure how to handle it. The wife said, 'No, this is how you should have handled it.' He yelled, 'Don't tell me how to handle it!' There was no way to escape. My seat was right in between them. A lot of their arguments came from one or the other's need to say, 'I told you so.' It was regular and daily and sometimes over really inconsequential things—who would go to the supermarket after work and such. I'm convinced half their arguments came from spending too much time together. They were constantly in each other's faces. They had no healthy separation. None of us on their team ever took it to a supervisor. These teams are very close-knit and you rarely involve management. And they did do their jobs. When I moved to a new team about a year and a half later, it was a relief." ♦

Don't share the intimate details of your romance will your office pals.

We are the first to cop to the fact that when we females fall in love we have the unfortunate tendency to call up every single one of our bestest friends and share all the details. They then follow the ups and downs of our new relationship with more rapt attention than meteorologists pay to hurricanes.

Girlfriend, it's fine to tell all your best pals about your newfound beau. But here's the catch. You cannot, cannot tell your best *office* pals anything more than the most basic details. Don't tell them whether he wears boxers or briefs. Don't tell them what really happened with his last girlfriend, the one from payroll. Don't share highlights of your getaway weekend at the drop-dead-romantic inn with the four-poster feather bed . . .

Why? Do we have to say it again? You're causing us pain here.

IM from ISpotAContradiction   X
Didn't you just say that it was necessary to keep your membership in the office gang active? How can I do this if I don't share at least some details about my new mate with my office pals?
Spot, are you saying that staying tight with the office gang necessitates telling them everything that's going on in your life? We didn't think so. Your office gang will likely understand why you're

keeping relationship details to a bare minimum. If someone keeps begging for specifics, plying you with questions, you might want to consider that this person is not really a friend but a competitor digging dirt to use against you.

Don't leave work together. Or worse, arrive at work together.

We admit that this can be something of a no-win proposition, especially if your relationship is known to your fellow staffers. They are likely to suspect you are up to elaborate shenanigans even if you did in fact spend the night apart.

When Stephanie and Tom got serious, they ran smack into this issue. No matter what they did or tried, they could not stop the wisecracks. They were frequently greeted with nasty frat-house-like jokes at almost every turn including—and we wish we didn't have to give an example here—"So how was it last night?"

There is only one solution. Don't arrive at work together. It makes you look like the senior class homecoming couple, not two professionals who would like to be taken seriously. If people are going to talk, don't add fuel to the fire. Soon it will be a bonfire, and then a wildfire.

Don't send love messages via office computers or office e-mail accounts.

Since you no doubt read Chapter 6 about how to indicate interest, we can only hope you are not surprised to read this directive.

But what you may not realize is that our e-mail ban holds throughout your relationship. We repeat it here for the same reasons as before. An e-mail sent in the office is not yours. It's not private. And your company's employee handbook might even say so in writing and may go so far as to prohibit your using e-mail for personal business as well. Even if your company is one of the rare ones with a policy of not reviewing its employees' electronic correspondence, you still need to be wary of your coworkers. Sound paranoid? Maybe so. But Helaine once worked at a company where a high-level employee was caught breaking into fellow employees' e-mail accounts and reading their messages. If this isn't discouraging enough, consider this gruesome quote from an online workplace chat board: "OMG! I was swapping pretty intimate e-mail with my boyfriend slash coworker and was pulled into my boss's office and presented with printouts of the evidence. Not good."

What's more, even your personal e-mail account isn't perfectly safe. Not because your colleagues are going to find a way to log into it, although for all we know that's also a possibility. No, it's because your personal e-mail messages are just as forwardable as the ones you write from your office computer. The police chief in Portland, Oregon, found himself demoted in 2006 after a former lover who worked as a desk clerk in the department accused him of various misconduct (later dismissed) and set off a media frenzy when she included his x-rated e-mail missives in public documents connected to her claims. He was demoted not because her charges held up but because the mere publicity involved made it impossible for him to command respect as Portland police's highest officer. The e-mails made it onto the Internet, where they will live forever, and we've seen them. They're nothing the former chief would have wanted us to see.

And he sent them from his personal PC, just like anyone in a relationship might not think twice of doing.

FAMOUS "DATES" IN OFFICE MATE HISTORY

2006 Congressman Mark Foley of Florida wins himself spots in both the Hall of Shame and the Hall of Stupidity when he is caught IMing lascivious messages to underage Congressional pages.

We haven't even mentioned the grisly possibility of clicking on the wrong recipient when you're attempting to send a covert message to your office honey. How many times have you pressed Enter after typing one too few of the first letters on your intended recipient's address when there wasn't anything much at stake, let alone when the consequences of the wrong person receiving it are so dire? Enough said.

We concede that this e-mail prohibition is a little sad. Stephanie and her hubby Tom, back in the MCI Mail days before present-day e-mail, sent each other notes many times a day and have a precious record of the beginning of their relationship. This was before it ever occurred to corporate America—or your average small-business owner—that they could poke about in your e-mail or IM logs. But it doesn't matter how delightful it would be to have an archive of love notes sent from your office computers. You can't have one.

If you choose to ignore us (and we suspect you might), we beg you to at least follow a few very simple rules. Keep it short. Don't make it graphic. Don't reference anything physical. Don't put down various colleagues or your boss. Don't write anything you would be mortified to have other people read. Don't write anything that could come back to haunt you. Try to limit your office correspondence to basic information sharing.

Don't hang around each other's workstations.

Your desk isn't like your locker in high school. It is a place of business. Are you allowed to say hello during the day? Of course you are. What we are talking about here is excessive visitations, sipping coffee, and sharing witticisms with your darling instead of other coworkers or, dare we say it, actually performing the job you are getting paid to do.

If your romance is not public knowledge, don't send "anonymous" display gifts on special days.

If you're an underground couple, presumably you want to stay that way. Sending anonymous displays, leading curious colleagues to play Office Jeopardy in an attempt to figure out who spent the money, is not the way to go.

In fact, lavish displays are definitely a no-no, no matter how well established a couple you are. Ditto squishy sentimental items like large stuffies. Did we need to say that? Again, you're attempting to look professional. As for more substantial gifts, make your presentation outside the office.

Can you ever send or receive a subtle spray of flowers? Well, we'd prefer you don't. But if your romance is out in the open, does not appear to be attracting negative feedback, and is not affecting your work performance, it might well be okay. It also depends on your company. If your organization is extra-friendly to office romance, you are likely on safe ground. And of course if your romance is so established that not sending flowers is more likely to arouse more comment than sending them, the path is clear. But short of that, can't you just send the flowers to home? Flowers look nice at home.

Don't engage in public displays of affection, however welcome, even at—especially at—the office Christmas party.

If we need to explain this one to you, we've done a lousy job so far. Let's just say your colleagues do not want to watch you making out at the Xerox machine. They don't want to see you enter an office together and shut the door. They don't want to see you paw your beloved after a few too many drinks at the annual holiday party. And if they do see such things, well, of course they are going to talk about them. And gossip about them. And make sure they tell everyone who wasn't there to witness the events themselves about them.

FAST FACT

A survey by WorldWIT, an online group for professional women, found that 61 percent of the 35,000 members polled said they have had an office relationship. There's more: 20 percent admitted to intimate acts in the office itself.

As for the ones who are above gossip—well, many of them will think less of you. After all, you've just demonstrated a remarkable lack of restraint and self-awareness. And that is not the behavior that gets people juicy assignments, as Sharon discovered.

WATER COOLER CONFESSION

"wild things"

"Will and I were working for the same skiing conglomerate in Mammoth, California. We didn't know each other well, but one day at an office outing we found ourselves on a chairlift. I was freezing and had forgotten my gloves. Will held my hands in his to warm them. We ended up having our first date on Valentine's Day, and that sort of set the tone from then on. We tried to keep our relationship a secret from our colleagues at first, but a few months later, during drinks after work, we ended up on the dance floor, and we went wild. The words *groped* and *French-kissed* apply. The next morning everyone in the company knew we were having a fling. That set the tone too—we each suffered separate layoffs when the ski resort company downsized. But we got engaged four years after our first date, and were married eighteen months later." ◢

Yes, we know all of this behavior, or lack thereof, requires a bit of discipline. But we know you are capable of it. All of these Don'ts demand a little discipline. But that's all right. Everything worth having demands discipline, including your job.

takeaways from chapter 10

1. Given the opportunity, people in offices will behave like the adults they are. So don't act like a teenager, all goony-eyed with looooove.
2. We don't think any more highly of using e-mail to communicate with your office mate than we did earlier in the book.
3. When you're navigating your interoffice relationship, try not to be your own worst enemy by broadcasting your relationship.

CHAPTER 11

When Do You Tell?

Not to Mention, *How* Do You Tell?

You and your office mate are in love. Life is wonderful. Work is wonderful. Should you tell your coworkers about your strategic alliance? We're not talking about your supervisor right now, we're talking about the office gang. Tell, don't tell?

A) Yes

B) No

C) It depends.

If you picked C, consider yourself a winner in the Helaine and Stephanie common-sense sweepstakes. After all, there are a few questions that need to be asked and answered before we can give you firm direction.

How public is your merger?

If you, um, "announced" your alliance by misbehaving at happy hour or at your firm's holiday party, you might as well be up-front with folks. It's not like they don't know what's going on if they witnessed you pawing one another. Your village mates are an inquisitive bunch, and they're not stupid. They are unlikely to buy any story about alcohol leading to a horrible, one-off mistake. They are more likely to subscribe to the old saying *in vino veritas* and scrutinize you and your new mate for any sign of a slipup— which you will no doubt provide if you are truly an item.

FAST FACT

Secrecy is becoming less common for office mates. Career-builder.com's 2007 survey found that only 34 percent of workplace daters kept their relationship a secret, down from almost 50 percent two years earlier.

What is your firm's policy on office mating?

If you work at a firm where your budding romance might cause trouble, you are likely to want to keep things on the QT for longer than you would otherwise. This is especially true if you work at one of the rare firms that bans office romance. You will have to behave, we hate to say it, as if you are dating your boss. Follow the guidelines in Chapter 12 and consider the possibility that you might have to choose between your relationship and your job.

What if your colleagues are a bunch of juveniles, hoping for the titillation of office romance to spice up their boring days on the job?

No need to be their entertainment du jour. Alternately, you might just decide to get the information out there, provide the masses with a few days of fun, and then bore them into dropping the subject. If you've read and followed the guidelines in this entire book your behavior will be so impeccable there will be nothing for them to gossip about after the initial revelation.

How old are you?

Later in the book we'll discuss the fact that twentysomething workers can get away with certain office romance behaviors that would seem far more inappropriate in someone older. Serial office dating is one (see Chapter 16). Going public is another. It stands to reason that if you are young and foolish, you will be forgiven for dating one office mate after another, and you will similarly be forgiven for telling people. But if you're older, there are multiple reasons to keep your own counsel, the desire to maintain your company's respect for your judgment being one of them. A survey by Spherion Corporation and Harris Interactive bears this out. They found that 57 percent of the youngest workers, ages eighteen to twenty-four, were completely open about their office relationships versus a mere 25 percent of their sixty-five-and-older colleagues.

Are you a stickler for privacy?

It's fine to feel that way. Most Human Resources professionals would agree your personal life is your own, as long as it doesn't interfere with your work. But know that it's unusual for both members of an office couple to feel the need to conceal the relationship indefinitely. If you get serious and you still want to keep your alliance a secret, your office mate might come to the conclusion that you're ashamed of it. Or worse, unaware colleagues might say something to you about your lover that you'd rather not hear. This situation caused bumpy times for Laura and Steve.

WATER COOLER CONFESSION

"mum's the word"

"We were in the same department but working on different projects. I guess you could say we were side-by-side coworkers. Our office was a pretty social group; we hung out together and partied together, and almost all of us were young and single. Steve and I became closer and closer. One night we left the office together when it suddenly began to pour. We ducked into the first shelter—which was an X-rated strip joint in Times Square! It was crazy and depressing but it bonded us in a new way. Nothing happened, but a few days later he sent me an IM: Would you like to have lunch with me? Well, we were dating after that. We managed to keep it a secret for two years. He was just adamant that his personal life was no one's business and I . . . well, I thought if we broke up it would be even more miserable if everyone knew about it. But I don't think I ever felt comfortable working with him in the same department side-by-side. It could get so awkward. I remember once someone complaining about Steve, going on and on and I just couldn't say anything. I internalized it and it made me miserable. I was so much happier when I moved to another department. Then we could tell people. But we never told Human Resources or our respective bosses.

One other thing: if you date and marry a colleague, be prepared to have a big wedding! There were a lot of coworkers we felt we had to invite because we met at work." ◢

The second unexpected reason to reconsider the privacy thing is that after a certain point, just because you think you are keeping a secret doesn't mean you actually *are* keeping one. You might just be surrounded by exceptionally well-mannered colleagues, hesitant to confront you and your office mate. As one woman interviewed for this book told us when we asked her if she knew any other couples we could chat with, "There are three couples in my office I would love to have you talk to but that would mean I would have to admit to knowing what is going on."

Interestingly, most of us might be inclined to assume that the more-private member of an office couple would tend to be the guy, as in Laura's confession above, on the theory that men don't confide about their love lives in the way women do. But that's not what researchers have found. Our friends at Spherion and Harris say that women are more secretive than men by a margin of 41 percent to 31 percent. The reason? Women say they fear the damage to their career more than men do.

FAMOUS "DATES" IN OFFICE MATE HISTORY

1669 The eventual Marquise de Maintenon, then called Mme. Scarron, was appointed governess to French King Louis XIV's illegitimate children. The secrecy shrouding their eventual affair and marriage was so successful that historians not only still debate if the couple's liaison began in 1673, 1678, or 1680, but also what year they finally married and what, if any, influence the Marquise had in French political life. This amount of secrecy is remarkable given the way they lived: French royalty was considered so exalted, the King could not even go to the bathroom with complete privacy.

And finally, there's the concern that secrecy can be erotic. Not that we're against heightened eroticism—we're all for just about anything that makes for high drama in the bedroom. But office romances, particularly ones that need to remain hidden, are by their nature tinged with drama. That can make it harder to divine whether they are solid and promising or blazing with short-term, soon-to-be-extinguished, fanned-by-the-flames-of-the-forbidden excitement.

A Final Note

Our advice: You might want to chat with your new office mate about whether and how you will tell people about your romance. If and when you decide to go public, it's certainly easy enough. You don't need to send out a company-wide e-mail. (You're not allowed to use e-mail anyway, remember?) Turning up together at a work-related evening function and leaving in tandem will probably do the trick.

takeaways from chapter 11

1. Just because you choose not to tell the office gang that you're dating one of their own doesn't mean they don't know already.
2. The more mistakes you made at the beginning of your office romance and the younger you are, the more you should consider coming clean.
3. Stereotypes don't hold when it comes to office romance—women are more likely to keep their workplace affairs to themselves than their male colleagues are.

CHAPTER 12

Dating the Boss or a Subordinate

Sometimes the Dos and Don'ts from Chapters 9 and 10 need to work overtime. He's a vice president. You're just starting out. Or you're a vice president and he's just starting out. Either way, you are spending more and more time together. Too much time together, actually. Now what?

Even in companies where office relationships openly flourish, management frequently finds the need to establish one no-crossing zone: boss/subordinate dating.

Yeah, yeah, you've heard it all before. There has hardly been an article written on workplace relationships that doesn't slam the possibility of enjoying a romantic relationship with the person responsible for giving your performance review and handing out assignments. The reasons a Human Resources professional or management consultant might object are glaringly obvious: complications can range from accusations of favoritism to charges of sexual harassment. Any promotion, salary increase, or award the junior partner in the relationship receives is likely to be forever suspect.

___FAST FACT___

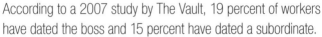

According to a 2007 study by The Vault, 19 percent of workers have dated the boss and 15 percent have dated a subordinate.

The heart, however, knows not from office regs and unwritten rules, and there are too many happy couples out there who violated this taboo for us to insist you not go there. After all, the situation is a staple of women's fiction from *Jane Eyre* to *Bridget Jones's Diary,* not to mention such brilliant oddities as the 2002 cult hit film *Secretary,* in which office assistant Maggie Gyllenhaal finds inexplicable enjoyment in a sadomasochistic relationship with her lawyer boss, James Spader. There is probably a good reason for the continued popularity of this evergreen plot device. Wish fulfillment, anyone?

Two Words That Can Make Dating the Boss Worth the Agitation

But given all the mess these affairs can cause, our wording in this chapter will have to be somewhat more romantic than in previous ones. Here goes. *There's only one reason to take the risk of dating someone you work for, or who works for you: True Love.*

We're not trying to make you chuckle here. We're being sincere. Don't attempt to date your direct boss or your subordinate unless you can picture the whole picture. We're talking marriage (or forever togetherness), the mortgage, the kids—the works. (In other words, unless you can picture a heck of a lot more than True Sex.) Nothing less is worth all of the trouble you can potentially get into if the relationship goes *pffft*, or if your overtures are rejected entirely (in which case you should reread the section on sexual harassment law in Chapter 6).

So let's take it on faith that your feelings for your boss or your underling are huge. They're the most you've felt, perhaps, for anyone you've ever met. In which case we hope you work for an understanding company, but if you don't, in the words of the classic TV series *Hill Street Blues*, be careful out there. That means that if you're the underling you have to be surpassingly cautious about making the first move, and if you're the boss, even more so. If you do manage to leap the hurdles with such grace that you end up with a viable relationship, there might possibly come a moment when you must inform upper management. And in many cases there will come a moment when one of you has to leave the company. It's a progression, actually. It goes like this:

- Think twice.
- Did we mention you should think twice about this?
- Having thought twice, make the most subtle move possible to indicate interest.
- If your advance is accepted, keep your budding relationship a secret like you've kept nothing else a secret since the day of your birth.
- Did we say you can't tell *anybody*?
- Wait until you're sure it's long-term love before coming clean to a supervisor.
- Then move—you, your true love, both of you, to another department or another company. Or at least another direct report.

Hey, we didn't say that cross-level dating was easy. Ask Jane Eyre what condition Mr. Rochester was in when she finally snagged him.

But we're getting a little ahead of ourselves here. You may not be *allowed* to make this hypothetical first move at your company. It may be a firing offense. Your company may have it in writing, in the employee handbook, that fraternizing outside the office with your boss or your direct report can get you terminated. As a commissioner for the Ohio Civil Rights Commission observed, "As long as office dating policies are applied equally to both men and women, they don't violate any civil rights laws."

FAST FACT

More than 90 percent of companies that do have a policy on office mate kissy-face forbid direct subordinates and superiors from hooking up, according to the American Management Association. But look on the bright side: More than 70 percent of companies have no written rules on interoffice dating at all, making it unlikely that your company has a formal policy forbidding you from romancing the boss.

Most companies prefer to dissuade employees from taking part in direct boss/subordinate romances. Take NCR, a *Fortune* 500 technology firm. According to their employee relations manual: "NCR strongly discourages employees from living with, dating, or becoming involved in a romantic relationship with another person over whom the employee has supervisory, hiring or disciplinary authority."

In the event that such an alliance forms, the manual goes on to say, "Managers/Subordinates who have entered into such a relationship are required to immediately disclose the existence of such a relationship."

Even companies that consider themselves especially supportive of true love on the job have been known to express a few quivers of worry at the prospect of boss-subordinate relationships. So we called the lovely folks at Southwest Airlines—you know, the ones who profile happy corporate couples in their company magazine—to get a few words of advice.

"When you have more than 32,000 employees, supervisor/employee relationships are likely to happen," admits Pam Anderson, Southwest's manager of employee relations. "But if someone reports to you, there should be no romantic relationship."

So how do you resolve this conundrum?

"Our expectation is that the employees will work it out by transferring jobs or at least their reporting roles," Anderson responds, adding that the protocol is that the senior corporate member of the relationship approach his or her supervisor about the relationship and work out what to do. "It's a leadership expectation," she adds for good measure.

But hey, many of us don't work at companies as *Office Mate*-friendly as Southwest Airlines. So let us put this idea forward: Not only should you be sure it's True Love, you should be sure you're willing to lose your job—and any future job that depends on a positive recommendation from your superior at your current place of employment—to have a relationship with the unequal colleague of your dreams. Unlikely? Yes. But it happens. Be prepared.

For the purposes of the rest of this chapter, we're going to assume that your company hasn't already promised, in writing, to can you for dating this much-desired creature. And let's assume you haven't already fallen into each other's arms without an overt move on either part. You've got to figure out how to make that move with dignity and precision.

I don't care how hard you've examined these issues, there is NO WAY to make a move on someone higher or lower than you that gets rejected without it feeling like harassment or without it ruining the harmonious working relationship between the two people.

- -

Break, you have a point there. In a way, the only approach you can make in a dating situation between people who are on different rungs of the employee ladder is a successful one. Every move that is rejected creates an enormous problem. That's why we strongly suggest you don't even make the attempt unless you are convinced it's True Love. We might add that you shouldn't make the attempt unless you are similarly convinced that your overture will be accepted. But given the possibility that it won't be, we need some serious ground rules here. Read on.

How do you indicate interest in a boss or underling? Well, just the same way you would indicate interest in any other coworker but much, much, much, more carefully.

Don't Come Out of Nowhere

We can only hope this isn't just your idea. We take it for granted that you two are flirtatious with each other. Or at least talking about things other than work. Out of such vibing, other things naturally follow. More or less, anyway. Any request for a romantic date—even one between people who met nowhere near the office and have no professional ambitions in common—requires a leap of faith and leaves you open to rejection and hurt. We can't take those two words out of the equation. But this is a time to attempt to analyze the cues in your situation as dispassionately as possible. This is no time for guesswork.

Don't Make Your Move in the Office, No Matter What Your Excuse

You two are working late into the night, and you are moving closer and closer to each other . . . STOP RIGHT THERE. If there was ever a time to step back and take a breath, this is it. Suggest going out for a drink after you are done. If that feels awkward to you, take it as a sign that maybe this relationship is not meant to be. Again, asking someone out on a date is a nerve-racking experience. Asking a subordinate or boss is triply so. We're sorry, but there's no magic potion you can drink to get around that fact.

Cautious Does Not Mean Coy

Earlier we said you need to be surpassingly cautious when you put the moves on your boss or subordinate. Cautious does not mean coy. Translation: you need to *telegraph your interest in the most direct but small, subtle way possible.* This way your cue will not be mistaken, but can still be deflected without ruining your good working relationship. You may not think this is the most romantic way of going about it, but it is the way most likely to save you grief and embarrassment if your intended does not reciprocate your interest for any reason.

> **Coy Example:** "I'm so impressed by the way you handled that client. I would have just curled up like a salted slug." (This would be accompanied by eyelash-batting.)

> **Non-Coy Example:** "I'm always impressed by the way you handle yourself in difficult situations. I'd like to find out more about you and your approach. Would you like to go out for a drink tonight after work?"

As you can see from the second example, the verbiage is direct and includes both work and non-work references. But at the same time, it's understated so that if the person who hears it doesn't want to go in that direction, they have an easy out. Which is why we say . . .

Leave Yourself Open to Rejection

Your subtle but direct move must be done with such confidence and adult aplomb that its recipient will understand that you make room for the possibility that they do not reciprocate your interest. You will not be vengeful, angry, sulky. Your enjoyable and productive professional partnership will continue to thrive. (And if it hasn't been an enjoyable and productive professional partnership, you have no business attempting to go on a date in the first place.) By knowing it is true, your manner will convey the reality that there is no *quid pro quo* here.

You're like a method actor at this point. If your romantic feelings are so big that you're willing to flout the boss/subordinate dating taboo, they're also so big that you want what's best for the person you care for. Truly believing these things will make them appear in your face. (If you're laughing right now, you have never either taken an acting class or watched Bravo's *Inside the Actor's Studio*.)

Make the First Move If It Feels Right to You

Speaking of *quid pro quo*, who should make the first move, boss or subordinate? Even we won't attempt to dictate that one. It simply depends too much on the circumstances and the individuals involved. While conducting interviews for this book, we heard both sides of the story. And what worked for those couples is no more than what worked for them. Sometimes, you just have to go with your gut, as Jack did.

WATER COOLER CONFESSION

"who's the boss?"

"I was a sergeant in the police force and Katie was an officer. I wasn't sure I'd ever get married or have kids. Katie certainly didn't look like a cop, with her long, wavy brown hair, careful makeup, and curvy figure. She ended up on the cover of *Parade* magazine, she was so pretty. Then I heard that she was available. I wondered what would happen if I gave her a rose at Christmastime. I wanted to make sure to give it to her outside the station, so when it was time for her to go home I went to stand outside. But I got her schedule wrong and I had to stay out there for ages before her shift finally ended. I gave her the rose and said, 'Merry Christmas.' Then I looked for an opportune time to ask her out but two or three months went by without my finding one. I was nervous being her supervisor, and there was a lot going on at the time about sexual harassment. She must have gotten tired of waiting because finally I got a handwritten note from her in my mailbox saying let's get together for a drink, and that was it. We went on a bowling date and then to the track, and got married two years later. We've been married for seventeen years and have three children." ♦

So let's say the move has been made and accepted and now you are a happy couple. Remember the first line of this chapter? We said that sometimes the Dos and Don'ts from Chapters 9 and 10 need to work overtime. We're not kidding. You know what this means. *Utter secrecy.* More discipline, more adult behavior, than you have ever exhibited before. *You cannot give yourselves away.* Perhaps we should rephrase that slightly. *You cannot give yourselves away until you have alerted supervisors to the situation.*

FAMOUS "DATES" IN OFFICE MATE HISTORY

1998 Now-former Enron CEO Jeffrey Skilling decides he wants to date fellow employee Rebecca Carter, nicknamed "Va-Voom" by her helpful coworkers. He seeks permission from the Board of Directors before making his move. Before giving their approval, they joke that perhaps the lady in question might turn him down. She doesn't, but now she might wish she did. They go on to marry, but her formerly high-up hubby is now serving a twenty-four-year prison sentence for fraud.

Even if you're successful in following our secrecy edict, we warn of a danger we've mentioned before, and that's the 007 thing. You need to embrace both the secret and the normal. You won't go out to dinner where anyone from work might see you (which means you may not be able to go out for dinner, at least not for the moment). But you really must hang out with each other's family and non-office friends. If you feel inhibited from doing that, say, because of your stunning age difference or inappropriateness as long-term partners, we hope this is telling you something. (That being: it's not really True Love. It's True Lust, May-December variety. In a word: Pygmalion.) Carmen found out what the non-normalcy of a boss-subordinate relationship can mean.

WATER COOLER CONFESSION

"good at work but not at home"

"I was twenty-three years old and my boss at our trade publication was eight years older. We went out for lunch one day after appearing on a radio show together. Over lunch he said he really liked me. I was caught off guard. There was no big first date; we just spent more and more time together. We worked at the same company for four years and never openly acknowledged it, but it was clear to the other employees that we were a couple. It was a small office, only five people, and things were definitely heightened. I regret that now. No one said anything directly, but they knew. It was a 'don't ask, don't tell' policy, and it wasn't good for the relationship. It made the relationship seem hidden and secret when it wasn't and it ended up affecting the relationship. We broke up." ◆

A Word or Two about Pillow Talk

Some hazards of office dating are heightened between a couple who work at differing levels. One of those is pillow talk. Most of us bring our workplace problems home. We tend to talk them out with best friends and significant others. We're only human.

But if you are involved in one of these relationships, pillow talk should be banned. Other people's careers are at stake here. If you're pissed at a colleague who pulled a fast one at the office and you're dating a jazz singer, you get to vent. But if you're pissed at a colleague who pulled a fast one and your lover has the power to fire the guy, your venting could have lasting implications.

Whether you're the boss or the subordinate, you are in possession of insider information. Budget cuts, corporate restructurings, schedule changes on the Christmas retail shift, questionable entries on a colleague's expense report, you name it. Not only are you risking sensitive information getting out (no matter how well-intentioned, who among us hasn't at least once inadvertently revealed a secret?), at any moment you could put your office mate in a dicey position. Even at the most benign level it's undesirable. Do you want to be the recipient of information pertinent to a friend that you can't tell them? However juicy the information, it's junk food. Once ingested, it'll make you feel rotten. You don't need it.

So if you are the lower-status half of the couple, don't dig for information. Don't ask who's on the rise in the corporate hierarchy. No peeking at secret salary negotiations or other interoffice communications. No advocating for your pal in receivables, who is arguing with a colleague over respective job responsibilities. You are not a latter-day Madame du Pompadour seeking to become the power behind the throne. Anything less than perfect behavior is going to allow your fellow villagers—we're speaking of your coworkers—to turn on you. And they will. Believe us.

Let's say that, in all innocence, you find out something you should not have. You glimpse a confidential memo on your honey's computer screen. Or you overhear an urgent call made to or from a cell phone off-hours. The best you can do is to put it out of your mind. Permanently. And that includes after the fact becomes common knowledge or after you and bossman or secretaryman have broken up. No telling colleagues, "Oh, sure, I knew Jane was on the layoff list six months ago." Sure, your fellow villagers will be impressed with your insider knowledge. But it's also likely that they will despise you for it. What else do you know? What other key information are you planning not to share with them? Remember how we told you earlier that you need to maintain your membership in the office gang, albeit with some discretion? It's time to remember that.

A Word or Two about Favoritism

It's ironic that people observing a romance between unequal partners often assume that one of the parties is looking for a leg up, because in reality the members of an unequal partnership can never accept help from each other of any kind. Just as the underling can't help her boss boyfriend by passing along a bit of office gang gossip, he can't offer her any workplace goodies and she can't accept them. As we said before, nothing less than perfect behavior is permitted here. If you're not inclined to comply, know that a 2005 California Supreme Court decision gives employees the right to sue for "sexual favoritism." What's that, you ask? Well, if an employee is sleeping with the boss and getting plum assignments as a result, coworkers can claim they've been the victims of sexual harassment.

When the top executives of public companies violate this rule, they can head right to the front page. In 1980 rumors swirled that William Agee, CEO of manufacturing juggernaut Bendix, was having an affair with his executive assistant Mary Cunningham. They denied the affair. He promoted her to vice president, and national headlines resulted even though she was a recent Harvard MBA who might very well have deserved such a position. They married two years later, so it's hard to imagine that too many people gave her credit for earning her promotion, no matter how well she might have performed.

FAMOUS "DATES" IN OFFICE MATE HISTORY

1976 Powerful Congressman Wayne Hays is revealed to have employed one Elizabeth Ray as a clerk in his Washington office even though she famously claimed, "I can't type, I can't file, I can't even answer the phone." Interestingly, the congressman had just married his longtime secretary, a woman named Pat Peak.

Let's say you fall into the category of the subordinate so often portrayed on TV who is getting involved with the boss as a means to further her career. Not that you would do such a thing. If that is your true motive, or even a piece of your true motive, you're better off remaining friends. You can exchange information with a friend. You can accept a friend's help in landing a prime assignment or in getting a promotion. You can't accept these things from the colleague you're sleeping with.

But if your heart is in the right place, you'll go out of your way to avoid the slightest hint of favoritism or the pursuit of favors. Just ask Barack Obama. After his first year of law school, he worked as a summer associate at a Chicago law firm. He fell immediately for his assigned advisor, Michelle. He asked her out. She said no. He kept pursuing her. She kept saying no, explaining that since she was his advisor, going on a date with him was inappropriate. So Obama offered to quit, and only then did Michelle agree to a date. He took her to Baskin-Robbins, and he later reported that their first kiss tasted like chocolate. As he told *O* magazine, "I had known those student loans were going to get me a great education, but I had no idea they'd get me my first date with the love of my life."

A Word or Two about Non-Direct Reports

What if the boss you love is not *your* boss? Generally, most regulations define boss/supervisory terms as two people in a direct-reporting situation. That doesn't mean, however, that employers are not concerned when the two halves of an office couple are on different supervisory levels, even if one doesn't report to the other. One never knows, after all, what the future might bring.

NCR, for example, leaves the disclosure of these relationships to the discretion of those involved by saying that if the budding partnership has the potential to cause a conflict of interest, it needs to be reported. However, a number of universities have taken a hard line on these couplings—at least when a student is involved. The University of California system, for example, forbids faculty members from engaging in romantic encounters with any student with whom they have or can in the future "reasonably expect" to have a teaching, evaluating, or otherwise supervisory relationship. Few people find a relationship between a professor and an eighteen-year-old freshman to be appropriate. Nonetheless, a number of faculty members have complained publicly about the policy as it also concerns older graduate students—pointing out that the term "reasonably expect" is a rather vague standard that might have resulted in a ban on their own past relationships that subsequently led to marriage.

A Word of Warning

We all know that when it comes to matters sexual, the world judges women much more harshly than men. And this goes for office dating as well. Unfortunately, men dating female superiors seem to be given the benefit of the doubt much more frequently than women in the same position. University of Connecticut professor Gary Powell found in 2001 that when MBA candidates were asked about a hypothetical romance between a senior-level executive and a younger, single, lower-level employee, they judged the situation more harshly when they thought the subordinate was female. All the more reason to be on your best behavior at all times.

Conversely, dating the boss might not be such a bad thing for guys. In a 2006 survey by Careerbuilder.com, 25 percent of men who dated a supervisor said it had helped their careers. Perhaps not surprisingly, only 13 percent of women agreed with that statement, leading us to conclude that sexism is alive and well in the modern workplace.

A Word about Informing Management

So when do you inform a supervisor about your newfound truest true love? As long as you won't get fired for it, inform someone quickly. *Very* quickly. Don't go running from your first date to the appropriate supervisor's office, but within a few weeks is probably the right timing. Definitely before any gossip slips out. And keep in mind, if there is gossip, you might be the last to know. Odds are your fellow workplace villagers won't come up to you and ask point blank about your romantic relationship with the head of the department. They are much more likely to speculate behind your back.

One exception to this rule is if you're on different levels at a company but don't have anything to do with each other in a business context. But that's the only exception we've got for you.

What if the relationship ends within a few weeks, before the point when you would inform someone official? Well, you probably don't have to go in and say *I had this relationship and now I don't.* Your supervisor is not your father, and you're not an eight-year-old who rode your bicycle in the street. But we say this while holding the belief that both you and your former beloved are rational adults, capable of taking a failed romance in stride (at least on the job). If you suspect your boss/former lover might get vengeful or junior deputy/ex-paramour might be so angry that he is willing to start making allegations, make an appointment with Human Resources. Fast.

But we know this is unlikely to be you. After all, you read the first part of this chapter, the one that warned you not to act in haste. And you didn't. Now you have a great job and a great love. Treat both with gravity and respect and you just might get to keep them.

takeaways from chapter 12

1. Even in companies with a friendly corporate attitude toward office romance, it's possible there is a prohibition against dating between a supervisor and a direct report.
2. Don't take the prohibition lightly. Your company means it.
3. There's only one reason to take both your heart and your job in your hands, and that is True Love.
4. We couldn't be more serious.
5. If it's really True Love, you won't have any trouble following the suggestions found in this chapter. How's that for a litmus test?

CHAPTER 13

Dating an Equal

Just in case the Office Mate of your dreams is your professional equal and you're wiping your brow with relief that you don't have to deal with any of the damage in the previous chapter, wait. Dating an equal often means dating the competition. Now *there's* a challenge. And it takes a few different forms.

The Direct-Competitors Couple

It's so easy to meet and fall for someone who does the same job you do. There are, thrown together relentlessly. From the moment you are hired you have an instant and ridiculous amount in common. You're probably close to the same age, with the same background. You make roughly the same salary. (As the gal, you might make a smidge less, but we won't get into that here. Why depress everyone?) If your supervisor is a troll or your colleagues are insufferable, you complain about all the same people. It's a match made in heaven.

Or not. As journalists, we've seen firsthand how rough it can be for two writers/lovers in the same pool—on the same beat, even—to compete with each other for a juicy assignment or a promotion to editor. And yet, an enormous number of couples who meet, marry, and continue working together happen to work for media companies. So it must be do-able.

FAST FACT

In 2006 the blog "LA Observed" published a leaked internal memo from the *New York Times* that mocked the ubiquity of its interoffice romances. In an announcement of newsroom promotions it was noted of one reporter: "And, as the ads might say, he got his wife through *The New York Times.*"

No matter how many couples make it work, however, we suggest you at least weigh the pros and cons of changing your situation instead. Here's why: loving a competitor can be a toxic soup for some people. Yes, there are folks who handle it with equanimity and grace. But why should you have to? Why put yourself in the position of dealing with what happens when one of you gets the assignment, the business trip, the raise, even the promotion, that the other wanted? Why live in a fish bowl, noticing your peers in the cube farm watch to see how you handle these crises?

We interviewed numerous people who found themselves in direct competition with a new paramour. Almost to a man (or woman) they said they wished they had been able to move to another department or company much earlier in the relationship.

And these were the folks with a ring on their finger! Many of the ones who didn't end up in a permanent relationship said they believed it all would have ended much faster had they not been coworkers. The fact that they worked so intimately with each other and so well together made it harder to make a decision to move on personally, if not professionally.

What's more, there aren't just issues of romantic competition involved. Oftentimes romance between equals can lead to cringe-inducing encounters with oblivious fellow employees who rant about your beloved if they feel wronged professionally. You can't jump to your office mate's defense and you can't choose that moment to reveal your alliance. You're left figuring out how to appear both neutral and sympathetic without actually saying anything more significant than "hmm."

So if you are uncomfortable sharing the same title as your honey, we have this to say: It's likely that one of you loves this job a lot less than the other. To continue using the example of our home planet of journalism, one of you considers this magazine/newspaper to be a compromise. You're both working at the *Armadillo Newsletter* where one of you has long dreamed of writing about porcupines. Maybe it's time to send your résumé to the *Porcupine Press*. Later, you'll say, "I'm so glad I met So-and-So back at the *Armadillo Newsletter*; I never would have gotten that fabulous job writing about the dangers of quills." After all, the saying "there are other fish in the sea" doesn't just apply to the opposite sex. It applies to jobs too.

But let's say you're both working for the factory/restaurant/public school equivalent of the *New York Times*. Or let's say you see nothing to be uncomfortable about. Either way, ain't neither of you leavin' nohow. That's okay. You can both stay and compete in this job that you adore. And when one of you gets a goodie and the other doesn't, pretend that your office mate is your best girlfriend, not your office boyfriend, and behave accordingly. There are few people in the workforce who would say that they haven't found a single real friend on the job. So chances are you've had to deal with work-related jealousy between yourself and a friend before. And when your friend got the goodie, you probably dealt with her as generously and maturely as possible—at least as far as anyone observing could tell.

So if your boyfriend gets the plum you've gone after, act as if your best friend—the one you want as much for as you do for yourself—had been the recipient. And if you can't treat your office mate as magnanimously as you would your best friend, you shouldn't be office-mating in the first place. This is supposed to be a relationship based on more than heat, remember?

You can do it. Workplaces are filled with competing office mates who have figured out a way not only to work together, but to work together well. Because you can believe that if they didn't work well together, no one would allow them to continue.

The Conflict-of-Interest Couple

Sometimes couples do not work together directly but are still in for a romantic rocky road. Why? Because others perceive their careers as creating conflicts of interest that raise ethical concerns. They've been making movies about these sorts of partnerships for decades—think of the classic Katharine Hepburn–Spencer Tracy film *Adam's Rib*, in which a husband and wife who both happen to be lawyers find themselves on the opposite sides in a murder case—but more often than not there isn't much funny there. Think about it for a minute: If you are in charge of, say, deciding on construction contractors for a housing firm, and you are dating a local plywood supplier who just happens to be bidding on the job, you can see where your boss and colleagues might suspect something fishy is going on.

Office mates working in politics can find themselves particularly prone to becoming a conflict-of-interest couple. Are you a high-end lobbyist spending your nights with a congressional aide? Rest assured some avid blogger somewhere is going to be keeping an eagle eye on every amendment your loved one's boss is adding to congressional bills, watching for a perceived slipup. A journalist dating a potential source? The *Los Angeles Times* published a story in early 2007 detailing the potential conflicts of interest of a number of prominent political journalists (including their own employees), noting the high-ranking campaign staffers to whom they are married.

So what is such a couple to do? That's a really good question. Our first bit of advice would be disclose, disclose, disclose. Don't try to keep your relationship a secret. Tell anyone you think might be affected by it. As for your own behavior, many of our directives in Chapter 12 on dating the boss apply here. Don't dig for insider information, try to avoid pillow talk, and keep your counsel. And, needless to say, don't give undeserved professional benefits to each other.

Be ye warned that one of you might have to step down from your job or change responsibilities. The *Los Angeles Times* banned a well-known political writer from covering the 2008 presidential elections because his wife was working as spokesperson for a Republican candidate. As press watchdog Tom Rosenstiel noted, "You have the right to marry anyone you want, but you don't have the right to cover any beat you want."

Some people attempt to preempt the problem on their own. NBC correspondent Campbell Brown's husband—a former Republican strategist—rejected job overtures from at least one political campaign and started his own business so that Brown could continue in her job covering politics for the network without facing conflict-of-interest accusations. Now that's a guy we'd like to meet!

The Mismatched Peer Couple

How about when the two of you are in the same profession—or worse, the same job, as above—and one of your stars is rising while the other's is falling? Definitely no fun at all.

It's one thing if you're at different workplaces and one of you can attribute your particular lack of progress to an evil boss, rampant sexism, budget cuts, whatever. But when you've got the same job and one of you is succeeding while the other is failing (or stagnating), it puts extra stress on your relationship. It's obviously possible to succeed in your office, as the fact that one of you is being promoted proves.

But this cloud is not without a silver lining. There's key information to be gleaned from this situation. If you're the one who isn't on the rise, wouldn't you want to figure out why not, even if the Star of the Moment weren't the person you're sleeping with? Maybe you need to ask what you're doing to cause this discrepancy. Or maybe you're doing nothing wrong but are in desperate need of a new supervisor. In that case, perhaps you should improve your prospects by finding an atmosphere more receptive to your talents, as Joan's future husband Mike did.

WATER COOLER CONFESSION

"ups and downs"

"I broke up with my college boyfriend right after I began a new job. One day I'm sitting at my desk and I get an IM from Mike, a guy working a similar job to mine but in another department. It said, 'Do you want to meet for coffee?' It turned out he thought I was beautiful and had heard I was dating again. We hit it off right away. But it was never simple. I'd just gotten promoted when he e-mailed me, but Mike was still waiting for his break. It took me a while to realize he didn't want my advice. He needed to resolve the situation on his own. But I respected his vision and I believed in him. Finally, just as his boss informed him that he didn't have a future where he was, he applied for a job in another department and miraculously, he got it. They have loved him to this day.

"I learned you have to ask yourself early in a relationship if the person is more important to you than the job. I knew that I didn't want to lose this guy. In the long run, it's just a job and no one from work is going to come visit you in the nursing home. For us, work tested our relationship and made it strong. When we got engaged someone sent out a companywide e-mail, and people stood up and applauded when they saw it." ♦

What if it's your office honey who is flailing and not you? This dilemma offers you some pretty useful information as well. Maybe you're thinking about committing to this person long-term. Is there something you're seeing that should make you take pause? Is your honey shooting himself in the foot or is he merely in a bad professional spot? You may want to factor all of this into any decision you make about how to proceed. Particularly if you determine that the fault doesn't lie with him, but you still feel the urge to bolt. This might tell you your office mate isn't someone so important to you that you are ready to help him through a difficult time. Maybe he's in the wrong career, and maybe the right career isn't quite as prestigious as his current one. If his job is part of the attraction, perhaps your attraction is more to his position than to the man himself.

Examine what the situation is telling you about your significant other. Examine what the situation is telling you about yourself. Then stop examining and act on this information. Information is a good thing, no matter how much pain you might have endured to acquire it. When it comes to dating someone you met at work, the extra information the arrangement yields can be your greatest asset.

The Frighteningly Well-Matched Peer Couple

Sometimes a couple who met when they worked together, even at the same job as competitors for all the same rewards, can thrive to an almost scary degree. They love the extra time they get to spend together. They speak their own language. They both have a gift for their work and their careers are moving forward almost in lockstep. They might even—like the publishing couples we know—get married, have children, and then continue working at the same company and sometimes even in the same department.

Well, that's just great. You think we're about to shoot a gaping hole in this picture, but why should we? Sometimes people simply work beautifully together. You might find them leaving their company at some point and launching a firm together. And yes, once in a while a pairing like this does blow up in a headline-making divorce. But other times the things that drew them to their vocation and to the same company also drew them to each other, and the chemistry continues to work year after year as with Lisa and Michel.

WATER COOLER CONFESSION

"he said, she said"

Lisa: "We were both newly hired for a consumer affairs segment on a television news program. Michel was the on-air legal expert, I was his producer. We were in a small department, in teeny cubicles next to each other. I wasn't exactly his boss, but I did have to tell him what to do. He was always semiflirtatious, always complimentary. I had no interest. I was dating someone else at the time."

Michel: "We were foisted upon each other. She was my producer. I was immediately attracted to her. She's a beautiful woman. Over the months the attraction grew beyond the physical. She's smart and feisty and we had spirited discussions about work."

Lisa: "It was the Christmas party. I went by myself and got there early. I started drinking Cosmopolitans by the bar, and by the time Michel arrived I was a bit tipsy. We were dancing with different people and I just went up to him and planted a big kiss on him, right in the middle of the room. No one could believe it."

Michel: "Our first date was the night of the office Christmas party. One thing led to another, and it became obvious this was a date."

Lisa: "We had a very liberal newsroom; there were at least four other couples. It worked out great. It was the best of both worlds. He was someone I worked with and he was my best friend. We were friends first. That was the key to our attraction and success."

Michel: "We got engaged on the anniversary of the Christmas party. At work, we were still separated by a divider. It was small—you could see our shoulders and heads above it. I know there were some people who thought it was odd, but there were several other couples on this job. There was a director and a line producer who had been together for at least eight years—they worked together side by side in a tiny control room. I think it was a testament to our original friendship—we were able to compartmentalize work and home."

Lisa: "We stayed together at the show for six years. Eventually our segments changed but we remained sitting next to each other and sometimes still worked together. Then he changed jobs . . . "

Michel: "I do miss working with Lisa. She's very good at what she does. She's so pretty and charming and she could always open doors. And once she got that door open, she had the skills and know-how to do the job and do it well." ◢

Of course, one luxury that the well-matched peer couple has—now and for the rest of their couplehood—is the ability to work together again, combining their strengths and enhancing both of their careers while deepening their marriage.

FAMOUS "DATES" IN OFFICE MATE HISTORY

2003 Indie rock band Arcade Fire is founded by husband-and-wife musicians Win Butler and Régine Chassagne, who met when she was performing jazz standards in Montreal. The band is considered an Internet phenomenon, gaining much of its popularity with little promotion and, at first, no actual CD releases.

The Battle-Scarred Couple

Who knew that the hostile conditions of the modern American workplace could be contributing to workplace romance?

We all hear the horror stories. Supervisors who rule by intimidation. Companies where no one knows who is going to get fired and when. Bully bosses who scream at their underlings. Workplaces where the hours are long and the breaks from stress are few and far between. It can be horrible on the cube farm. But the horror is sometimes mitigated by the soothing effect of the love matches that it can inspire. Or, maybe the lust matches it can inspire. Think of it as an employee benefit not mentioned in your new-employee information packet.

How can this be? Being terrorized is an objectively bad thing. But several decades ago, a professor had the lovely idea of subjecting two clusters of college students to different teacher behavior. One group was subjected to a nasty tirade about how badly they had performed on an exam. Nothing was said to the other. They were then asked to write a story. Guess which group's tales included significantly more sexual content?

Other researchers over the years have confirmed the theory: The more frightened a person is, the more likely he or she is to become sexually aroused. Our personal favorite is a study titled "Love at First Fright." A picture of an "average attractive" man or woman was shown to a person of the opposite sex either just before or just after they got off a roller-coaster ride. The subject was asked to comment on the looks and dating potential of the guy or gal in the snapshot. Those asked about the photo after they exited the ride found the subject in the picture much more desirable than those asked about the snapshot before their trip into faux terror.

Is this you, and if so, is that a problem? It could be if you're looking for something more than survivors' lust. The battle may have brought you together, but it can't be the thing that keeps you together. So examine your relationship in its everyday state. You want to make sure your main topic of conversation is not your awful boss and his or her truly misguided and Machiavellian management techniques. Hopefully your conversation extends beyond the toxic dynamic of your dysfunctional office gang or the icky culture so warmly embraced by your firm.

Remember, good things *and* bad things can bring office mates together. But bad situations can't be the only things *keeping* you together. It won't work, or anyway, it won't last. You should enjoy your time together, not survive it.

—*takeaways from chapter 13*—

1. You're not sleeping with your boss. That doesn't mean you have no worries worth mentioning.
2. It can be just as tricky to go out with the competition as it is to date your supervisor.
3. When you work with someone, you get to see firsthand why he or she was passed over for that promotion. Don't ignore this information. What if your partner never performed any better at work—would that be a problem for you?
4. Love can be frightening, fair enough. But don't be frightened into it.

CHAPTER 14

Don't Go There,
Or No, No, No

There is an exception to every rule, but you're probably not it. We say this with love.

Some of the things we are going to talk about in this chapter might sound obvious. Others you might disagree with vehemently. You'll read our prohibition against dating a married colleague and think something along the lines of:

"Well, my married boss had an affair with his married counterpart in accounting and nothing happened to them but a bit of embarrassment at the company Christmas party when they had to introduce their unaware spouses to one another."

Or you'll hear that we consider in-office hanky panky off-limits and protest:

"But Malkie in the mailroom had a quickie on the sorting table with a fellow delivery mate and her supervisors never found out."

Yes, many people get away with many things, but to assume you will be one of them strikes us as courting paycheck disaster. Or *you* might get away with something touchy, but that doesn't mean your office mate will get away with it too.

So without further ado, here is our list of things to please, please, please keep out of the office and off the job. We don't cite them because we are stuffy Puritans. We don't cite them because we don't want you to have fun. We don't cite them because we don't like you very much. We want you to live long and prosper. Prospering generally involves continuing to receive your salary. Plus, these activities give office mates everywhere a bad reputation and we are all about promoting the interests of office mates. So listen to us. Now and forever.

Adultery

Firms can ban office romance. They can ban boss-subordinate relationships. But they can't ban adultery. The reason: In all but a handful of states, such regs would run afoul of laws banning discrimination on the basis of marital status. But don't think you are safe. Firms can still get you on charges of inappropriate workplace conduct.

So let the married CEO have an affair with someone else. Let the married *anyone* have an affair with someone else. And the same goes for you if you are married. (Why are you looking for love at work if you're married, by the way?) Take your unhappiness with your chosen life partner elsewhere.

Be practical for a minute: If you get fired or otherwise disciplined for the fallout of an inappropriate relationship in the office, how on earth do you expect to explain the resulting imbroglio to your spouse? Conversely, if your spouse finds out about the affair and demands you leave your job to save the marriage, how do you explain your sudden departure to your boss?

Aha, you are thinking, *I'm not the one who's married. It's my inamorato's problem*. First off, that's a pretty selfish attitude to take. But leaving aside the morality here, know that the stink of an interoffice adulterous affair has a way of clinging to everyone involved. Know that the world has a way of judging the woman—whether she is the married partner or not—more harshly than the man in equivalent positions. Know that the end of the affair is unlikely to feature you and your new office mate riding off into the sunset—and if you do, there will likely be lawyers to pay. Don't believe us? Ask Jack Welch.

There are so many unforeseen consequences of adultery on the job it would be impossible to list them. Let the following confession from Glynnis suffice.

WATER COOLER CONFESSION

"truth or consequences"

"I got married at twenty when I was totally unformed. It was just what people did at the time. I ended up being hired by a man who was starting a new agency and needed someone with writing skills to help him launch it. It was a very exciting time and we worked together intensely every day doing things we'd never done before. Then we'd go out for drinks after work. He was married too, but he came on to me. I rebuffed him. After about a year I gave in. The affair went on for about ten years, nine of which we worked together. He would beg me to marry him but I never considered it because it would have upset so many people. I got pregnant by him and my son is his son. I think my husband knows but we've never talked about it. My son is twenty-five now and he would love to have siblings and a family—his real father has two grown daughters—but I just don't know how or if to tell him. My fantasy is that my husband is on his deathbed and I say, 'There's something I need to tell you,' and he says, 'I knew that.'" ♦

We know we risk sounding naïve here. We know office mating has a way of, well, *happening* to some married people. Hell, we've seen it just *happen* in most every office we've ever worked in. Stephanie must own up that the handsome older man she dated was married when she met him, and she suspects that the only reason her reputation didn't suffer was that she was let off the hook for being young and foolish. Office mate canoodling among the married set is so regrettably common that a therapist we spoke to while writing this book assumed we would be writing primarily about adultery. In fact, The Vault discovered that 33 percent of employees say they know a married coworker who has had or is having an affair. So at the very least you know you'll be the subject of gossip; if people are tattling to The Vault, they've got to be tattling to each other.

This kind of story is so juicy that it can take on a life of its own. The players and their managers are powerless to stop it. When a senior manager at a firm Helaine worked for left his wife for a fellow employee, the gossip got so nasty that junior workers were actually instructed to stop discussing the situation, a move that predictably backfired.

FAST FACT

In 2006 Halfpriceperfumes.co.uk found that 15 percent of respondents to an Internet survey admitted to cheating on their spouses with a colleague.

So at the very least, know this: Your fellow colleagues will happily swap tidbits over the situation for *years* into the future, no matter how your affair resolves. We've told such tales ourselves. And the more damaging the details—poor pregnant wife, children, overheard phone conversations, lovebirds spied in compromising positions—the more buzz. Here's another one from Helaine's back files. When she was househunting a few years ago and told the real estate agent the name of the company where she was working at the time, the agent inquired about an, um, situation she had heard was taking place in *Helaine's* village. Word really gets around. And if you don't believe us, take it from Patrick?

WATER COOLER CONFESSION

"cheating myself"

"I was married and working incredibly long hours—seventy-plus a week—as the manager of a chain store. I'd come home and just want to sleep, but my wife would want to talk or go out or something. Things were deteriorating at home. We had a bunch of management interns at our place from a local community college. One day one of the young ladies came in wearing a sexy lacy dress and looking really hot. Without thinking, I said, 'You look very pretty in that.' One thing led to another and within a few weeks I offered her a ride home one night. Well, we didn't make it out of the parking lot for over an hour. We began to meet before and after work and within a few months we both quit our jobs and moved in together. As it turned out we didn't have much in common. We eventually split up and I went back to my wife. But I still hadn't learned my lesson. I took a job as a manager with another chain. It was a very flirtatious atmosphere.

But someone must have reported my behavior because one day the district manager showed up. He watched me for an entire shift and then fired me for favoritism. As for my wife, we eventually divorced. I can't say enough how much I regret my behavior. I allowed office romances to rule me." ◊

We write all this knowing that many adulterous workplace situations end with little or no professional harm to anyone involved but for some embarrassment. But, again, why take the risk? This is both an emotional and employment minefield, and consequences can be severe and lifelong.

FAST FACT

When your fellow employees are all of the opposite sex, your chances of divorce go up 70 percent. Moreover, divorce itself is its own risk factor. A third of your fellow opposite-sex office buddies split up lately? Your chances of ending up in the same boat increase by almost 50 percent.

In-Office Hanky Panky

You might also try to avoid having sex with anyone, married or otherwise, at your workplace. You never know where the security cameras might be.

FAMOUS "DATES" IN OFFICE MATE HISTORY

1998 Monica Lewinsky. Bill Clinton. The Nos involved are unending. They begin with the cigar thing, end with the dress thing, and include just about everything in between.

And even if security doesn't catch you, don't assume you are safe from your colleagues. Want to be the one caught in the act when your boss remembers he left a really important document at the office? And decides to go fetch it at 1 A.M.? How about when one of your coworkers gets you on cell phone video and shows it around to the gang the next morning?

The Vault, a career information organization that conducts an annual office romance survey, found that nearly 20 percent of all office denizens admitted to in-office trysts in 2007. They reported that top trysting locations include one's own office, the restroom, the elevator, copy room, and supply closet. A few brave souls even utilized their boss's office for their romantic interlude.

You'd think the above rule goes without saying, but there's obviously a titillation factor in risking getting caught for some people. Or just in doing what is forbidden.

Conference Hanky Panky and Other One-Nighters

Conferences are frequently viewed as the equivalent of a singles bar for the office-bound. You get to go to an event, often far from home. You leave your day-to-day life behind, including bullying bosses. You are surrounded by people who share an enthusiasm for a subject that is likely to be of some interest to you. There are numerous opportunities for socializing, especially after hours. So is it wrong to hook up with someone in this setting?

Pretty much.

For one thing, we here at *Office Mate* don't support office hookups. That prohibition includes folks you meet through work either on or off the premises. It covers people from your office that you might indulge with while away on a business trip, and people in your industry who don't work for the same employer but who are attending the same industry function. If you're looking for a one-nighter, don't go hunting for it where you work or at a business-related function.

If you are reading this book, the chances are you are searching for a more meaningful relationship than one that lasts a night or two. Phew. So the question you need to ask yourself here is, "Do you think this relationship has a future?"

In other words, if you meet someone at a conference, you need to make a quick assessment, something we've spent most of this book arguing against. This isn't as daunting—or con-tradictory—as it sounds. We are simply asking you to think whether there could be something there. If the answer is yes, act like someone who has read *Office Mate*. Find out if there's some-thing behind the physical attraction. Don't jump the hottie's bones. Let the conference be the first chance you have to get to know this person better. Have lunch. And/or dinner. Exchange business cards and make sure to get his business *and* personal e-mail. Stay in touch and see what develops. Our advice is similar if this is a mental attraction. If you and this person can't stop talking to one another, remain open to the possibility that there might be something here that will have a longer life than just a conference contact.

But if you're from Dallas and this guy flew to the confer-ence from Vancouver, and he's Canadian, and his whole family lives within a five-mile radius of him, and you can't imagine ever moving to Canada, it's probably not going to work out long-term. In which case it would be the smart thing to walk away rather than work out between the sheets for one glorious night.

As for a one-nighter with a married guy who is taking advantage of the distance from home, come on. You know how we feel about this. Aside from the moral issues involved, this is trouble you could spare yourself.

All that being said, if you indulge in a one-nighter during a conference—whether the guy is single or married—keep it quiet. Please make sure your colleagues don't catch you in a compromising position. And for God's sake, don't do it again. You deserve better.

But let's say you're on a business trip with someone you've long had your eye on back on the cube farm. Let's say you find out that he feels the same way about you. And let's say this could be the beginning of a beautiful office mateship. You have to exchange the first kiss somewhere. Where better than in the romantic setting of a luxury hotel where your company is footing the bill?

Broadcasting Trouble

There are other inappropriate forms of sharing your office mate woes besides public arguments. Like confiding in colleagues about the less-savory elements of your relationship with the man they thought they knew—that is, until you disabuse them of the notion. Even if you swear to yourself you won't do it, a beer or two at happy hour has a way of loosening a person's tongue. So much so that you might be tempted to turn to the nice woman sitting in the barstool to your left, the one who works across the street from your firm and feels like a safe haven, and unload on her. Are you so sure she doesn't have friends in your company?

On a bad relationship day, venting might give you a dose of relief, but it won't make you any friends or earn you any respect. It'll make you a Greatest Hit at the water cooler the next morning, that's for sure. And it might actually get you fired (inappropriate behavior, remember?). Take Tess's story as a cautionary tale.

WATER COOLER CONFESSION

"crushed"

"It was my first job out of college, at a branch office of a large public relations firm. He was a section head, more than a decade older. It was just hearts and stars from the moment I met him. I didn't care that he had a girlfriend; I was fired up with the power of love. I would wake up thrilled to go to work. Well, one night we were alone in the office together, and you can imagine the rest. My immediate boss found out and called me in and asked what was going on. I thought she was asking in friendship. I learned too late she wasn't. Another boss actually called me into her office and told me I was disgusting.

"My crush never left his girlfriend for good. It finally ended for us when he stood me up one day. I called his house and his girlfriend answered the phone! I said how-could-you, and he answered like it was a regular office conversation. 'Yeah, that's great,' he said. 'We'll talk about it tomorrow in the office.' I was in complete shock. I confronted him everywhere. In his office and in elevators. I told everyone what he had done to me, figuring if I was going to be humiliated I might as well control the flow of information. Finally, I was laid off. It was very clear this sort of behavior was not acceptable. I learned my fellow workers were not my friends. It was heartbreaking." ◗

Idiotic Moves Using the Newest Technology

We thought we had heard everything until an employer told us he had just fired one of his best employees because she had a work friend-with-benefits take 300 naked photos of her using a corporate client's next-gen cell phone. She was asked to use the phone as part of a buzz marketing campaign. That was during the day. At night she got hammered and engaged in said naked photography. Yes, she did "erase" the photos before she returned the phone to the client. But although the photos were deleted from the phone's picture log, they remained on its memory stick.

> **FAST FACT**
>
> A Canon Copiers UK survey revealed that just under a third of its service calls over the holidays were to fix problems related to replacing glass or clearing paper jams that "revealed evidence of embarrassing images." Such photocopies included a man's groin and a woman's very recognizable rear end. What made it "very recognizable"?

When the boss told her with honest regret that he was forced to fire her in order to preserve his relationship with his biggest client, he started the conversation with, "What were you thinking?" and ended by telling her that the only reference he'd be able to give her was to confirm that she had indeed worked there.

Not Taking No for an Answer

Speaking of No-Nos, no means no. Period. There's a legal term for ignoring this one. It's "harassment," and you can be sure your angry now-former friends in Human Resources will have something to say about it. And while we're at it, no stalking someone who has said "no." Sending persistent e-mails after hearing "no" is harassment. You're not allowed to send dating-related e-mails anyway. Remember Chapter 6?

As for those of you on the receiving end of a romantic overture, if you happen to be *playing* hard to get in the office, as opposed to actually *being* hard to get in the office—that is, sending a "no" message that you intend to turn into a "yes"—do office mates everywhere a favor and think of another game to play. Preferably elsewhere. Find a tennis court or something.

What Makes for a No-No?

You don't need us to keep going down the list mentioning every conceivable No-No we can think of, do you? You know which activities the No-Nos are. They're the ones that distance you from your all-important office gang. They're the ones that make you redden when you walk in the elevator in the morning. They're the ones that make you dust off your résumé because you know your tenure has come to an abrupt halt. Must we continue? Must we, for example, mention cigars? No cigars.

When Bad No's Happen to Good Workers

You swore no cigars, you dry-cleaned the clothes in your working wardrobe whenever they got dirty, and you crossed the street every time you saw that absolutely gorgeous unhappily married executive coming your way. And yet, somehow, you've engaged in a No-No. Can this reputation be saved? Yes and no. The answer depends on variables like how public your misbehavior may have been and how forgiving an environment your office/village may or may not be. Some of the starring players in our Famous "Dates" got that way because their mischief landed them on the front page of *The Wall Street Journal*. Not good at all. But odds are you have not met this fate. This is one of the few but tangible benefits of not yet having become an international business sensation.

So your misdeed is not known to millions. Thank God for small favors. But is it known to everyone in your department? Everyone in your company? Even if it's known only to you, your partner in crime, and your supervisor, you might well have to leave the company if you want your career to keep moving forward. It can be hard to bounce back from certain "Nos"—that is, if your supervisor is not related to you by blood. If he's not, say, your dad.

Now, if the only people who know about your transgression are the members of the office gang, you should be able to accomplish some damage control. There's only one way to do this. You have to back up. Move the gang back to the point before the Incident That Shall Not Be Named took place. Take the following steps, in order:

- Pick the office gang ringleader (you know, the one who would answer the question "Who am I talking to?") and explain how mortified you are.
- Then shut up. Permanently.
- Wait until the ringleader has done his or her thing and spread the word about what you said.
- Never mention the incident again.

- Hold your head high and behave as if you are not actually capable of such behavior.
- Actually become incapable of such behavior. How hard can this be? You shouldn't have done it in the first place. You don't want to go through this damage control thing again, do you?

What we're saying is that you have to treat the incident like spilt milk. You can do this because you've figured out that only your posse is the wiser. Or maybe your dad is the wiser. But either way, the incident is recoverable; you can keep your job afterward. So the way to proceed is not to fall all over yourself in front of anyone who will listen and bellyache about how horrified you are that you were caught making out in the supply closet/smooching your married boss at Chez Fini/sneaking out of the anteroom of the Oval Office.

What if you thought you had contained the damage but you're confronted with an appallingly accurate recitation of your sins by a friend from a competing company at the next industry conclave? You can't adopt the innocent person's agitated, offended, rambling denial; even though an innocent person can't shut up, when a guilty person tries it they only sound more guilty. You can't seem unsurprised; that'll make you look guilty too. So, Miss Manners–like, we suggest the following cool riposte: "Lord, you're the third person to tell me that story! It's amazing what a rival will say to try to put a dent in your reputation." Smile your most charming smile.

Another variation on this: Laugh and walk away, head held high. If you say anything, limit it to something on the order of, "How amusing!"

The strategy common to both these responses: Never admit to anything. Don't lie but don't admit the truth, either. Your inquisitor is likely looking for some kind of reaction they can then share with their fellow worker bees. Don't give them one. And then

Don't.

Do it.

Again.

takeaways from chapter 14

1. Someone out there gets away with everything. That some-one is probably not you. Nor someone related to you. Nor someone going out with you.
2. When it comes to your misdeeds, your office gang is not composed of true friends. Don't confide in them.
3. Your tarnished reputation might one day be shiny again even if you engage in an office No-No. But do you really want to find out? Can't you date the married CEO of some company other than the one where you work?

CHAPTER 15

When He's Out of Your Life
But Not Out of the Office Next Door

The first guy Stephanie dated at her postgraduation job was an aspiring artist who worked in the art department. After a few months she realized they didn't have enough in common outside of work, but the artist—call him Jaz—fell seriously in love. Eventually Stephanie broke it off, and he took it hard. A few weeks later she noticed people at the office staring and whispering whenever she walked past. She discovered that Jaz had brought his oversized paintings to the office so that one of the staff photographers could take photos of them for Jaz to send to galleries. The largest painting, leaning against a wall for all to see, was a swirling orange and pink canvas filled with symbols of the failed relationship, including a blown-up version of her signature from a greeting card she'd given him: "All my love, Stephanie." There was nothing for her to do but try to gracefully ignore him and hope the office gang would do the same.

Oftentimes it's not the romance that forces you to leave your company/village, it's the breakup. The end of the affair can cause the most even-tempered person to become irrevocably separated from his common sense. And that's doubly unfortunate when it comes to workplace love. It's as crucial to keep your head *after* the relationship is over as when it's still going on.

FAST FACT

One in ten workers claims that an office romance drove them to leave their job, according to Careerbuilder.com, although the study didn't define how many of those left for positive reasons, like to get married.

Aside from getting one or both of you fired, a messy split can fracture your power base—no colleague, no matter how sympathetic, wants to play mediator. Or you can be seen forever as damaged goods, someone incapable of keeping her personal problems out of the office.

But we think you can survive this. Plenty of people do.

How? It depends on when you got your hands on *Office Mate*. Was it early in the relationship or late? If it was early, you behaved beautifully while the romance was in bloom. You didn't spend your time hovering over your lovey's desk, mooning over his every memo. You didn't leave with him at night or arrive arm in arm in the morning. It means that now that your merger has failed, you haven't become embroiled in a prolonged battle. You're not the talk of the company. That's because you discussed with your partner—back in your salad days—how you would conduct yourselves if things didn't work out. If this is the case, your path is clear. Continue behaving with the dignity your former amour has grown used to seeing in you.

But let's take a step back. Some of you haven't broken up yet and hope you never do. Some of you, unfortunately, see the end coming and are wondering how to handle it. Still others have broken up, perhaps disastrously, and you're coming to this text late. So, what should you have done, or what should you do now?

First, if you decide your office mate is, in reality, office waste, try not to tell him so in such blunt terms. Choose the reasons you give for ending it very carefully. Be tactful and under control. What you say today either fuels your future ex's soon-to-be-uncontrollable rage or sets the tone for a civilized ending.

Reasons to Give Your Office Mate as to Why It's Over

Good Reasons
- You think the two of you make a terrific team at work, but not as a couple.
- You are concerned the relationship is jeopardizing your professional stature.
- If you're dating someone much older or younger, you see the age difference causing troubles down the road.

Bad Reasons
- I met someone else.
- You don't listen to me.
- I hate the way you . . . (fill in the blank with something highly personal and specific like "shovel food into your mouth" or "miss the toilet when you pee").

Now, write down the real reason you are breaking up here.

_____

Good. Now that you've gotten that out of your system, choose a reason your soon-to-be-ex Office Mate can live with, and stick to it from this moment forward. Don't show anyone else this book. If a friend wants to borrow it, offer to buy her a copy of her own instead.

Rejection by E-Mail or IM

It came to our attention while writing this book that some people are using e-mail to break off workplace relationships. No, we don't mean they are writing screeds, telling their former office mates exactly what they think of them in graphic terms. What they're doing is not writing anything at all. The office mates in question are using e-mail response times to indicate the status of the relationship.

Here's how it works. When a couple is flirting or otherwise hot and heavy, the answers are fast and frequent, the virtual equivalent of witty repartee in a blockbuster romantic comedy. But when one party decides to send their office mate to the circular file? They take their sweet time in answering. Sometimes they don't respond at all. Ever. This strategy appears to be particularly common among office mates who indulged in one-night stands or the 9½ *Weeks* equivalent.

Our opinion: We can understand taking more time than in the past to answer your partner's e-mail when the relationship is waning. But to hope someone takes the hint and goes away without another word or act? Were you raised by wolves?

If you're going to break up with someone, at least have the courtesy to do it in person. E-mail silence isn't even a particularly effective strategy. We heard several stories from people who were flummoxed and made furious by sudden virtual silence. Frequently it led to more-prolonged discomfort between the twosome than would have resulted from an open confrontation. And if that doesn't stop you, think about this: How would you like to be on the receiving end of this tactic?

Of course, we write all this knowing you were thinking of employing an e-mail response blackout only from your personal account. On your home computer. Because if you've read this book you know very well you aren't supposed to be communicating via e-mail with your beloved office mate on a corporate computer or account—even if your wedding happens to be scheduled for this weekend.

What If You're the Rejectee?

If you're on the receiving end of a rejection, behave as you would hope an ex of yours would if you were the one delivering the bad news. Be calm, graceful, generous. This is especially important if your romance was public knowledge. Your colleagues are likely to be quite titillated by the tales of your failed liaison and any subsequent misbehavior. They will thrill to every twist and turn. And then they are likely to remember every mortifying lapse—whatever your excuse—for a *long* time to come.

IM from Heartbroken   ✕

```
I just can't help myself. I want to scream and cry
all the time over losing this office mate of mine.
Why should I kill myself trying to hold it all in?
I've already been humiliated—now I just want my
side heard.
```

Heartbroken, you met in the office, yes. But you
have to keep your breakup outside of it. We know
relationships often end with much screaming, cry-
ing, and slamming of doors. But when it comes to
the workplace, try, try, try to avoid such activities. Slam your apartment door, not your office
door. Cry to your childhood friends, not your
coworker friends. Practice deep-breathing exer-
cises at your desk. We know it's tough, but you'll
be a lot sadder when you are sans boyfriend and
sans paycheck. We know you're bleeding. But don't
bleed all over the office.

Things You Should Never Ever Do No Matter How Badly Your Ex Broke Your Heart

When you're wounded, your judgment is impaired, and
we acknowledge that. So perhaps we should really spell
out the behaviors we're asking you to avoid so there are no
misunderstandings.

Cry at the office. You can't hide it, not even if you have a
door to close, not even if you escape the bathroom. You're going
to look like a wreck and you'll be perceived as one. Breathe
through it. Cowboy up in public, fall apart at home.

Put members of your office gang in the line of fire. We can't
say this enough: do not confide in fellow employees. Especially
if they are also direct reports of your boss. Yes, you can mention
that your romantic relationship has ended—and you might if your
partnership was common knowledge—but keep it bare bones.
Don't sob to your fellow supermarket clerks about the floor manager who has turned out to be a wretched slimeball. Don't tell your
fellow inmates in the cube farm about the secret creep wearing

Armani suits in the corner office. Don't go above your former lover and spill his secrets to a supervisor. And if your ex has a secretary or assistant, don't ask him or her to intercede by putting in a good word for you. Above all, don't peck about for insider information, as in, is there a new squeeze in the picture? You don't want to test the loyalty of a person whose paycheck depends on it.

Refer to the situation in office e-mails. You don't need to start leaving a paper trail now. Don't write to your ex about anything other than workplace matters. No begging messages, no pleading to be taken back. No virtual arguments that go on for hours or days. No notes to fellow employees, badmouthing your now-hated former squeeze. If you need to vent to friends who work elsewhere, do it from your home computer. And write in Sanskrit.

Start dating someone else in the office on the rebound. It would be best if, having dated within the office with less-than-stellar results, you waited before attempting to find love in the workplace again. And when you're in that new relationship, be good enough to tell your ex what's going on so he doesn't suffer the humiliation of hearing it from someone else.

Call Human Resources, unless you are the victim of genuine harassment. Human Resources is not a psychologist, social worker, or (pre-)marital therapist. These people are there to hire, fire, and schedule maternity leave. If they wanted to hear about breakups, they would have become couples counselors. The only reason to contact Human Resources is if you had previously informed them of the relationship. In that case they have a right to know it has ended. And when you mention it, do so with grace and goodwill.

Quit in a huff. Whether verbally or in one of those dramatic letters left on a desk overnight. If you can't take being there anymore, try like hell to line up a new job. A great one. You don't want to go from one bad situation to another. Be patient. Not only will you get a better new position that way, you might well decide after three months you don't have to leave after all. If you do decide to go through with interviewing, don't tell prospective employers the real reason you decided to move on.

The list of self-sabotaging things office exes do just goes on and on. We don't mean to assume *you're* the guilty party. It doesn't always take two to tango when it comes to postbreakup misbehavior.

A Few More Idiotic Moves Ex-Office Mates Make

- Asking coworkers to choose sides.
- Giving filthy looks in the hallway.
- Returning personal items while at work, as in, walking through the door holding a large box bursting with boxer shorts.
- Asking to be assigned to a team your ex isn't on.
- Dating your ex's boss as payback.
- Exacting revenge of any description, as in trying to prevent your ex from being promoted.
- Public acts of destruction.

When You're Not the One Who's Behaving Badly

What if it's not you who is behaving badly—your ex, perhaps, or the office gang. How do you deal with them?

First, the Ex

You couldn't control your ex's behavior when you were dating—you can't control *anyone* else's behavior, whether you're dating them or not—so you're certainly not going to be able to control it now. As psychotherapists say, the only behavior you can control is your own.

So once again, we need to tell you to be unfailingly gracious and controlled. Even you didn't know how gracious you could be. Again, channel Miss Manners—why would you acknowledge someone who is behaving poorly? They simply don't deserve your time or attention, let alone your ire. You're above it. If your ex gives you pointed nasty looks in the hallway, smile like Mona Lisa. If he confronts you in the four walls of the office, act as if somebody is listening (heck, they probably are). Say, "I'm sorry, I'd rather not discuss this now. Let's find a better time and place." If your ex asks to be moved to another work team, do not react. Again, you're above it. Your ex asked to be reassigned? Funny, you hadn't noticed.

Then, the Office Gang

Intrigue-wise, it doesn't get any better for them than when two of their number break up with each other. Dissecting every detail certainly has a way of turning Wednesday into Friday in short order. You can't really blame them.

But you won't beat them, and you absolutely must not join them. That doesn't mean you should stand apart from them. Then your ex might get custody of the office gang, freezing you out, and we can't have that. That's like ceding the friends and neighbors to your ex in a divorce. In a divorce you'd have to leave town and start over to rebuild your social life, and in an office you'd have to find a new job. Why should you find a new job? You're not the one who's being childish.

So you'll resist the impulse to hang back from the office gang. You might even initiate the march to happy hour a couple of times just to signal your intention to stay in the mix. People will feel comfortable with you if you make them comfortable. It doesn't matter whether your ex is dishing out the gossip or not. Remember what we said earlier: no colleague, no matter how sympathetic, wants to play mediator. As fascinating as your ex's rantings may be, ultimately your gang wants to be left out of it. They will gossip, but that's the extent of it. Even that gets tired after a while. They've got better things to do, like work.

IM from OfficeFriendship   ✕

I can't apply this to my situation. My best friends are all on the job. If I didn't tell them why my former main man and I decided to toss each other into the circular file, they would never forgive me. Or tell me their personal secrets. Or work secrets. Ever again. I can't suddenly go all discreet and not give them at least a few bullet points about the latest doings in my personal life.

- -

OfficeFriendship, dear, you shouldn't have been telling your platonic office mates about your romantic relationship with your ex in the first place. But now that the harm is done, don't compound it as the relationship is ending. Don't bring up or allude to the subject yourself. Answer any direct inquiries with a polite smile and say something nebulous like "Yes, we are both satisfied with how the situation has resolved." Don't bite your lips and let your eyes water or otherwise show distress. Change the subject. Go all classy on them. Eventually they'll respect it, not resent it.

What If Your Former Love Is the Boss?

How should you handle giving the romantic pink slip to the person who signs your paychecks or annual evaluations?

Carefully. Give him a solid, identifiable, concrete-but-not-overly-personal reason for your conclusion, something objective that isn't easily fixed after you've pointed it out. The ones we gave earlier in this chapter will do nicely. Then, no matter how your manager/lover reacts, no matter how angry or anguished he becomes, you do not relent. You do not backslide and take him back for a final fling. You do not overreact. You do not engage. You are kind, warm, and neutral. What you are trying to accomplish is to get relations between you to return to the point where they were when you knew your boss only as well as your colleagues do. This does not mean you remain friends— not with the boss. With a colleague who is a former office mate you might, but not with the boss, not now. Perhaps you'll eventually find your way to a friendship, but that's for later.

FAMOUS "DATES" IN OFFICE MATE HISTORY

1536 Anne Boleyn. That's right, Henry VIII liked to meet women on the job, and Anne was the lady-in-waiting to his first wife, Catherine of Aragon. She dated the boss, got the big promotion, and paid for her mistake by suffering the biggest demotion in Office Mate history—execution by beheading. In fact, Henry was a serial office dater who met three of his six wives when they served as attendants to their predecessors.

Why is this point so important? First, your coworkers need to know you no longer have any special "ins" with the head honcho. Even if—like a good office mate—you never took advantage of your special access, there are those who are going to think you did or could in the future. So it's important to go back to being an average workaday employee. Not to *appear* to go back to being one, actually to go back to being one.

Moreover, disentangling yourself entirely from your boss postbreakup eliminates the possibility of there being any lingering unpleasantness over the affair. We all know how hard it is to maintain a true friendship with an ex when the affair occurs out in the real world. But when it occurs in the office fish bowl, it's particularly hard to finesse relations after it's over. So it's better not to have any. Do we mean forever? No. Just until you regain your standing with the office gang and define yourself again as you, not So-and-So's bed partner.

So when you're breaking up you tell him that you will remain friendly and positive in the office, but you do not actually remain friends. Note: You do not *tell* him that you will not remain friends. You just don't remain friends.

What It Means Not to Remain Friends with Your Boss/Ex

- Have an absolute minimum of interaction both within and without the office.
- Don't chat on the phone for any reason but business.
- Don't meet for the occasional drink.
- Smile in a friendly but neutral manner when you pass in the hall.
- Do not avoid opportunities to speak or work together, just as you do not look for opportunities to speak or work together. Allow for only the contact that comes naturally given your positions at work.

What if you didn't find *Office Mate* in time? What if you and Boss Man are the talk of the floor? What if your relationship is the first thing all new employees hear when they are taken out to lunch by the old employees?

That's all right, because it's about to change. The fact that you're breaking up with the person who may have diminished your prospects at your current company is about to be a thing of the past. A youthful indiscretion (if you're youthful). Something you're going to laugh about lightly a few months from now when one of your coworkers brings it up, because the fact that someone has mentioned it means they feel safe to rib you about it, and that's the moment you've been waiting for: the moment when you're one of the gang again and not The One the Boss Dated.

How do you get back on track? First, you end the relationship in as classy a manner as possible, as we have discussed. And you will follow through by returning to whatever behavior you observed in the presence of the boss before he knew the location of your rose tattoo. What will be different will be your behavior around your colleagues. You will let them come to you.

Remember, you have created a considerable distance between yourself and them by flaunting your romance with not just your boss, but their boss as well. They have come to resent you. A lot. You may not have noticed when you were in the throes of your dramatic love affair, but now that you're single again you will.

It's going to take a while before your colleagues will be ready to let you back in the fold. So you're not going to try to force your way back in by spilling all the insider secrets you uncovered under the boss's covers. And you're not going to start asking for help on your current project. Nobody wants to do you any favors, not for a while. You're going to be self-sufficient, upbeat, and constructive. If you've been confiding in a few office friends until now, you're not going to keep it up. You're just going to tell them the relationship is over, that you're fine, and then you're going to drop the subject. When they bring it up, you'll reiterate that you're relieved it's over, and drop the subject again.

Evidence That Your Coworkers Have Come to Resent You

- Group conversations come to an abrupt end when you approach.
- When you put down your tray at a lunch table, people find they are through eating and need to return to their desks.
- People avoid you at quitting time (so that they won't have to invite you to join the group for happy hour).
- When you try to come along to happy hour with the gang, suddenly everyone realizes they're tired and would really prefer to go home. When you walk away, they reassemble.
- On team assignments, you're always the last one to be asked for your expertise. Or to join a team in the first place, like in junior high school.

Getting the Romantic Pink Slip from the Boss

Sometimes you are going to find yourself madly, passionately in love with someone who no longer feels the same way about you. And, yes, sometimes that person will be your boss. But we know you can handle it. As we said earlier, no in-office scenes, complete with dramatics that would put the characters in a Latin American telenovela to shame. No speeches in front of the staff about how your now-former lover is really incapable of doing his assigned job. You might feel satisfied for a moment, but afterward you're stuck dealing with the aftermath. You have enough to deal with as it is. Instead, tell said lover that you accept that the relationship is over, and reassure him that you will take the high road at work and you know he will do the same. But once you take the high road, you have to keep walking it, as Phoebe found.

WATER COOLER CONFESSION

"on the rebound and out of a job"

"I dated my superior. But after two years he broke up with me. I wasn't happy, but I coped with it. I didn't weep all over him. I didn't spill to the rest of the staff. I also didn't see a problem when a coworker began to show interest in me, and I didn't see why I should keep my new romance a secret. Guess which two employees found themselves amongst the dozens getting the axe during a recent company-wide layoff? Let me tell you, sending out résumés together is not romantic." ◗

Does Your Broken Heart Mean You Should Leave?

These aren't the only possible permutations after a breakup: you behaving badly; your ex behaving badly. Maybe nobody is behaving badly, but you have a broken heart. For real. Why wouldn't you? You were friends with this person before you got involved. It felt like the real deal. You had more invested, most likely, than if you had met in a bar or on a blind date. So your heart might well be shattered. Perhaps there's nothing else to do but leave.

We're not saying that if you're not bouncing right back you should have to find a new job. We're just saying you can. You don't have to stay there and look at the back of your ex's head during sales meetings for the long and interminable foreseeable future. You don't have to listen to rumors that he's found somebody else. Sometimes an ex in your workplace is just too close for comfort, no matter what the reason. It's okay to acknowledge it and leave.

Signs You Should Switch Jobs after a Breakup
- More than six months after the event, you still can't focus your mind on work.
- More than six months after the event, you still haven't recovered the status quo in your relationships with your colleagues.
- It's clear your boss is aware of what's gone on in your personal life.
- It's clear your boss is aware that your work has been affected.

There are two ways to accomplish this. The first is that you can ask to be transferred—to another city, to another branch, to another department. (And take note: you can use this solution whether it's because your heart is too broken to stay or because your situation is too broken for you to stay, whether because of your ex's bad behavior, because of missteps on your part, or because of some other unforeseen outcome of a workplace breakup that can't be solved with the two of you in close physical proximity.)

Here's when you can ask for a transfer to another city/branch/department: when you can think of a legitimate reason why it's in your company's best interests. Isn't that how you get anything you really want in your career? You make your goal the solution to somebody else's problem. So do it. Tell them that you know the sales team in San Francisco just lost a key person and you've always wanted to live in San Francisco. (This would work especially well if the latter happens to be true. Why not realize one of your dreams while you're solving that other problem?) Point out that there's an opening for the position you've been aiming for in the branch across town. Explain that the Paris office hasn't started using the software you wrote. How can you feel sorry for yourself while living in Paris? Think of the Frenchmen you can date once you get there.

IM from HadEnough   ✕

Now I've had it. That is stupid. Just a few pages ago you said that an example of poor behavior in an ex is if he or she asks to be moved to a different team, but now you're saying it's okay to ask for a transfer? Don't you think if things are so bad that you need to ask for a transfer that you should just get it over with and find a new job?

- -

Had, we're talking about the difference between petty vengeance and a genuine solution to a genuine problem. When your ex asks to be moved to a different team immediately after a split, that's often just the adult version of a tantrum. You can practically hear the nyah-nyahs. But when you really can't work where you are, whether it's because of your ex's bad behavior or because of your irreparably broken heart, a transfer request may be in order.

Out of Love *and* Out of a Job?

There's one last matter to address. Unfortunately, you can do everything right, handle everything including the breakup with the utmost professionalism, and *still* find yourself out of a job.

While this stinks no matter what scenario got you there, it is a particular risk if you date the boss: sometimes you misjudge the character of a person with an unfortunate amount of power over you. There are vindictive bosses who will ratchet up the job demands, trash talk you to other supervisors, and make sure to quibble with everything you do until you are so miserable you decide to move on. And even then you won't get peace: Your former inamorata might not be willing to let things end. One common tactic: giving a bad reference.

If you find this happening to you, first try to talk to your former office mate about the situation. Tell him you understand he is unhappy with how things ended, but that this is not appropriate behavior. Point out that it reflects badly on both of you, that people in the know will suspect him of not being able to separate his emotions from his work. Stay calm. Do not let the conversation deteriorate into a postmortem on your romance.

One thing you can't do to solve the reference problem is to mention the embittered boss/ex in your interviews. There's just no way to win—you're raising too many questions in the interviewer's mind about what is essentially a he-said/she-said situation. This is another reason to look for a job while you've still got one. Tell the interviewer that he can't tell your boss that you're looking for a job without jeopardizing your career if the opportunity doesn't work out. Then give a rock-solid reference from your previous job plus a (trusted) peer recommendation from your current workplace. Better yet, give a reference from a supervisor at your current company whom you no longer report to or whom you worked for on a discrete project—if, of course, you have such a supervisor on your side.

If this doesn't get you past your boss's bad-mouthing, whether inside or outside the company, you might need to get the big guns. Reference-checking services will send a cease-and-desist letter on your behalf, demanding an end to all false comments. And of course there's always Human Resources. And defamation lawsuits. But if you continue to refuse to engage with your defamer, you'll significantly reduce your chances of getting to this point.

Remember, breaking up is tough. But so are you. You'll survive, even if it doesn't always seem that way. And you will find love again. Maybe even in the office.

takeaways from chapter 15

1. Most people survive office romance breakups.
2. If you thought you had to police yourself while dating an office mate, that's nothing compared to what you have to do after you break up with one.
3. Anything that makes you re-evaluate your career and act on your goals is worth the pain, even if the pain comes from an office mate breakup.
4. Every bit of advice we've given you goes double when breaking up with a boss.

CHAPTER 16

Serial Office Dating:
Possibly Inevitable but Not Necessarily Lethal

Nobody said you were guaranteed to get it right the first time. Tom was Stephanie's third workplace fling. Matt was Helaine's second (not counting an office lothario who made a pass at her at a Christmas party). It's not how many colleagues you date (okay, it sort of is), it's how you conduct yourself that determines whether your reputation will suffer as a result.

There's one other thing that determines what will happen to your reputation if you date more than one coworker, and that's your age. Serial dating is the one aspect of office romance in which youth has its privileges. The same factors that make the office the modern-day village are even more applicable to employees in their early twenties.

You're straight out of school. It's your first job. If you had a college sweetheart, the distance and the change in circumstances have made that partnership go sour. You might be in a new town or city. You have no life. All you've got is the other young people in your new office, and young people will hook up. And then unhook. As we said in the last chapter, spilt milk.

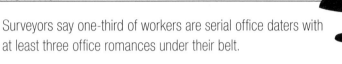

FAST FACT

Surveyors say one-third of workers are serial office daters with at least three office romances under their belt.

But the thing that has made you take office romance a bit too lightly—your youth—is the thing that will keep your serial office dating from killing your career (or your future at your current place of employ, anyway). The people who are above you on the totem pole know how young you are. They're likely to cut you a break. They certainly did for Stephanie. When she announced that she was leaving her first workplace to take a job at *Fortune*, her colleagues gave her two farewell parties and her supervisors took her out to a fancy lunch. But remember two things. She left. And she married that third guy—Tom.

Stephanie did one more very important thing right, however inadvertently. She did not ask that her office gang change allegiances when she did. And this is crucial. If a serial dater demands custody of the office gang with each breakup, you've all lost. Remember, you're a group of twentysomethings. All you've got is each other. If your romantic mergers and acquisitions involve splitting the group according to who's sleeping with whom, it's going to make Friday night happy hour a near impossibility. Not to mention fracturing what tiny power base your green little cohort might have established. The information you trade with each other is key to moving your nascent careers along—why shut down those channels with stupid struggles over allegiances? When you're launching your career *and* your love life, it's got to be all for one and one for all. It's a trap Anna-belle avoided nicely.

WATER COOLER CONFESSION

"fling after fling"

"When I moved to New York City, I made a resolution not to look for yet another boyfriend. This, it turned out, made me extremely attractive. I had minor flings with three guys in my office within six months. I never had any formal breakups with these guys. There would just be a signal from one of us to the other. Like, there was this one attractive copyeditor I saw for a little while. We would e-mail one another funny messages on the internal system and then, when the relationship slowed down, we would take a half-day to respond instead of answering immediately. When I started seeing someone else, the copyeditor ribbed me a bit but nothing too nasty.

"There was this one guy who was so funny and wonderful, but he was engaged. We would go out to lunch together. One day I said something that he misinterpreted to mean that I found him unattractive. I had to explain that if he weren't engaged I would be much more vocal about how attractive I found him. A few nights later I get this call at 1 A.M. 'I have to see you right now, I can't stop thinking about you.' It was so exciting, but the next day he was really cold to me. That was it for our lunches. Mercifully he worked in a different part of the building so it was less awkward than with the copyeditor, who sat near me. I guess I was his final fling before his marriage. He was certainly my last office fling, period. I must say, even though none of these was 'the one,' they were all rewarding in one way or another, and, in the bleak single years, were much more gentle and nourishing than the ghastly three-night stands I had on the dating circuit." ♦

So for the moment let's assume you're young and thus able to date more than one person in your office and live to tell the tale. Here's how you avoid getting a rep from serial office dating.

- Don't let anyone know you're dating someone in the office in the first place (then they won't notice you're dating yet another one).
- Keep any new alliance under wraps until it is very serious indeed.
- Try to avoid hookups. That's what singles bars and the Internet are for.
- Don't date someone who works too closely with your office ex.
- Don't date someone who is close friends with your office ex.
- Two people per department, max (and don't break up with the first guy before reading Chapter 15).
- End things gracefully (or take rejection well yourself).
- Keep things collegial between you and your former office mates.

Remember that when it comes to serial office dating, you can get a reputation even if you don't work in the office where you're dating, as Jennifer Aniston's character found out in the cult-favorite film *Office Space*. The restaurant where she worked was a romantic wasteland of the type we will discuss in Chapter 19 (they made her wear flair, for one thing), so she followed one of our suggestions—to find a connection to another office with better prospects. Unfortunately, she took our advice a little too well, as her new boyfriend discovered when an eager colleague assaulted him with an unappetizing list of her previous conquests in their office.

So whatever the office, after three workplace relationships you should either get married or give serious consideration to finding another workplace. But we suspect you won't do either of these things. Why? For the same reason you managed to get yourself into the pickle of having dated three people in the same office. You are either very young (this would account for Stephanie's lapse) or you're not actually looking for love. Just because you're young doesn't mean you can blithely disregard our discussions about the gravity of office romance. You're supposed to use the office to find the real thing, not to find hookups, remember?

IM from PartyGirl   **X**

Wow, you make romance sound about as fun and spontaneous as an enema. How controlled do you expect a person to be? This is passion we're talking about, not accounting.

- -

Actually, Party, this is your career we're talking about. Your career comes first. We never said otherwise. You can feel whatever you feel——don't get us wrong. But you're at work, so you can't do whatever you want. You need to show some discipline and restraint. The whole point of this book is to acknowledge the very compelling reality of the modern workplace——that it's the modern-day village and you will find more than just a paycheck there. You'll find a life, you'll find a love. But you do have to keep your job while you're looking.

Three office romances can be cute. Wild, crazy, silly—the goofy mistake you make because of your pathological youth. But no matter how young you are, four just sounds sleazy. And five . . . well, we'd rather not go there. We don't want you to go there either. One note: these numbers are proportionate to the size of your company. When we say three office romances can be cute, we're assuming you have chosen your three paramours from a large pool of candidates, perhaps in different departments. If there are only three eligible men in your office and you date all three of them, then no, that's not cute at all.

Youth Has Its Privileges

Now on to the post-twentysomething crowd. Beginning at some point in your early to mid-thirties, multiple interoffice romances will make you look worse than sleazy. They'll make you look pathetic. Especially—and unfairly—for women. An older man in an exalted position who dates a series of pretty young things can look like a stud. Sometimes a sad sack, but just as often not. A woman either looks like she's sleeping her way to the top or prioritizing her personal life over her career. And given the higher hurdles women have to leap to get to the highest corporate positions even today, you don't need your peers (and that's often who the bosses are if you're an older worker) coming to that conclusion.

But this book is about finding love in the office, not about avoiding love in the office. We're not saying older workers can't find love at work, we're just saying they won't get away with serial dating in the office with ease. But that's okay, because serial dating, when you're older, tends to happen when you're open to finding sex in the office rather than love. You're forty-five and on a business trip and you fall into bed with an attractive married colleague. That's not love. You're fifty-one and can't take your eye off your thirty-eight-year-old assistant, even though you know it could never work long-term. You end up having an affair anyway. That's not love either. Do you see where we're going with this? Go back to our edict in Chapter 14. It's true love or bust for older workers. Wait for true love and you won't become a serial dater.

FAMOUS "DATES" IN OFFICE MATE HISTORY

1762–1796 Reign of Russia's Catherine the Great. The empress appoints many of her lovers to official government positions, including longtime partner Grigory Potemkin. His attempts to impress her by supposedly erecting hollow facades of villages on the lands that his military campaign had won give the world the term "Potemkin Village."

That said, even an older employee can get away with a second interoffice relationship (second, not third) if the first was failed true love. Everyone, whatever their age, is forgiven for putting their heart on the line and having the misfortune of it not working out. If you date and marry an office mate and one day find yourself single again, you can go out and look for another one. Observers will even root for you. Nobody wants you to be alone forever, even if you divorced your first office mate.

So you can date one person, break up, and then date another person even past your thirties. It's just that the down time between relationships needs to be longer. And that's fine, because your discipline is even more likely to get you what you're looking for than for the twentysomethings who can better get away with serial office dating. A 2007 Spherion Workplace Snapshot survey conducted by Harris Interactive discovered that older workers are more likely to report that their workplace romances culminated in marriage than those under thirty. The older you are, the more impressive the numbers—among workers age sixty-five and up, 45 percent married their office mates. Age has its privileges too.

takeaways from chapter 16

1. If you're going to date one colleague after another, better stop at three and then either change jobs or get married.
2. One easy way to avoid serial office dating: NO HOOKUPS.
3. You can get away with serial office dating a little more easily if you're right out of school, but don't push it.

CHAPTER 17

Should I Stay or Should I Go?

Or, Leaving the Village

It's going well. It's going *really* well. Now what? Should you keep your job and try to rise as half of an established office couple, or leave? It's not difficult to suss out your office's attitude toward couples—watch how they treated the ones who came before you.

At her second magazine job, Stephanie watched a couple meet, fall in love, get engaged, get married, and continue to work together throughout—with both of their careers as healthy as they were the day they first saw each other. They adopted a baby and the wife went on maternity leave. It almost seemed like the company was a part of the couple's extended family. The way it was for that couple is how it can be at the most receptive companies, and if your workplace is one of them you probably already know it.

But even if it is, that doesn't mean both of you have to stay. You may not want to. Many of us—perhaps most of us—need or want some separation from our significant other, no matter how harmonious the relationship. You might be one of them. And having figured this out, and having evaluated the possibilities for achieving separation within the same workplace that we outlined in Chapter 15, you might not be able to solve the problem that way. One of you might have to leave the company altogether.

FAST FACT

A 2001 Swedish study found that working in the same office as one's spouse actually decreased chances of divorce by a startling 50 percent. Our thought: perhaps being observed by one's spouse would tend to reduce the urge to flirt with colleagues other than the spouse in question.

That's okay. The fact that you're in a long-term relationship with a coworker doesn't have to hurt your career. Even if—for whatever reason—one of you has to leave. Job-hopping, especially when you're in the datingest age group, is commonplace. According to a recent survey by business management professor Charlotte Shelton, the average employee in his or her twenties changes jobs between five and six times.

Earlier in this book we wrote about how to decide which of you should be the one to leave. We repeat: Rare is the office couple in which both partners are equally passionate about the job. The fact that your relationship means one of you has to leave could create an opportunity. Submit your résumé to that firm you've always wanted to work for. Take a chance and see if your graphic arts experience might wow them at Pixar. Find out if you could use your juris doctor to teach law instead of practice it. Make lemonade.

The Conversation

If having this conversation about who should make the sacrifice—especially if it *is* a sacrifice for one of you to leave—makes you squirm, think about why. This is not an easy discussion to have for anyone. But then again, your extra measure of discomfort might indicate your relationship is not serious enough to require the conversation. In that case, you shouldn't be having it, not at this juncture. We're talking about when your relationship has progressed to the point in which you are committed to each other and to your future together. Depending on how long you've been dating, the conversation could be one of the first in which a decision is made that will affect the two of you as a "we," not you versus your office mate. But it's only meant to be had between two people who are ready to speak on those terms.

FAST FACT

Halfpriceperfumes.co.uk found that of those who met their long-term partner in the office, just 6 percent of them were still working together.

If you're not serious enough to decide which one of you should leave but the nature of your workplace requires a change simply because you are dating at all, revert back to one of the other options we noted in Chapter 15. See if one of you can switch divisions, departments, branches, functions. Change the paradigm enough to get your supervisors' minds off your relationship and back on your performance. And don't say that you're asking for the switch because of your romance. As we've said before, make your move the solution to somebody else's problem.

Hello? You're telling me to consider giving up my job for love? When was this book written, 1907?

- -

Gal, we're not telling you to give up anything. We're saying you might come to this point to satisfy your own needs (as in the need for some space from your mate) or because of a management decision that forbids you to work together. You made the decision to date someone in your workplace and now you've fallen in love. There are consequences. Your relationship has brought you to the point where you have to figure out whether you will be able to continue working at the same company while growing your careers. Would you rather pretend all of this isn't happening or would you prefer to be proactive?

The nature of your company will likely have an impact on your decision. It's easier for work couples to make a go of it when they meet at large companies, and it's not hard to see why:

- Bigger offices mean you are less likely to see your office mate every two minutes.
- Bigger offices mean more opportunities for lateral transfers to other departments or divisions.
- Bigger offices mean enough middle management so that you might be able to report to different bosses.
- Bigger offices mean larger and more-sophisticated Human Resources departments, which usually have experience handling workplace romance.
- Smaller offices mean less physical space—which means little separation.

- Smaller offices mean it's harder to hide your shifting romantic moods from colleagues.
- Smaller offices mean if you can't work together—or your firm doesn't allow it—one of you will have to leave, and quickly.
- Smaller offices mean political and conflict-of-interest issues are more likely.
- Smaller offices mean no Human Resources department to mediate difficulties.

Office romance is one circumstance in which a big knotty conglomerate is actually a friendlier environment than a small, homey office. Somebody should tell Dilbert. Alexandra wishes somebody had told her too.

WATER COOLER CONFESSION

"caught outside and kicked out of the company"

"I got a new job at a small marketing company as a junior executive where Jim was in senior management. We had to work closely together on a particular account. It was nights and weekends and during the day we were all over Los Angeles taking meetings together. One night we went out for a beer after work and suddenly I knew Jim was the one. Soon we were dating, but we decided not to tell anyone since technically he was my boss. We were extremely careful for three months, ordering in food, watching videos, and going to restaurants in out-of-the-way neighborhoods. We always left the office at different times. Then Jim decided to take me to Santa Barbara for the weekend as a surprise. It was January and rainy and cold, so we thought we were safe. But as we were walking around we heard someone call our names. It was the head partner of the agency! By Monday everyone knew about us. It had always been a competitive and resentful office environment, but it had never been directed at me until now. It was toxic. There was no other direct report for me to move over to. When the head partner decided to give everyone on Jim's team a raise but me, I knew it was time to send out my résumé. What made it worse was that we were a great professional team. Our client was thrilled we were dating; she said we gave 150 percent to the job. But it didn't matter. Only our head partner's opinion mattered, and he was not happy. We're married now and I'm quite successful in my career, but I'd still tell anyone who's dating someone at work that it can turn ugly quickly, in ways you'd least expect." ◗

We don't want to be complete naysayers here. Sometimes a small office can work to your benefit—especially if you are the employee who ends up in everyone's good graces when things go awry. Not that we condone the *Office Mate* guideline-flouting behavior of Kelly, below.

WATER COOLER CONFESSION

"dumped and stiffed"

"Mike and I were editors at a small publication in a cheap industrial park in the suburbs. There was a great atmosphere in the office. We were all close, but I became particular friends with Mike. We would go out for drinks after work frequently. He'd talk a lot about his ex-wife, whom he had just divorced. He really wanted to get away and finally he managed to talk our head into opening a one-man office in Asia. The office organized a goodbye party at a local bar. Someone put Sinéad O'Connor's song *Nothing Compares 2 U* on the jukebox, and I just went up and told him that's how I felt about him. In the month before he left we had this intense affair. It really should have been a fling, but we had been close friends and it got really emotional. I kept it a secret from the entire office. He left in September and we planned for me to visit at Christmas. I bought a ticket. A few days before I was to leave, he left a message on my machine saying not to come, that he had met someone else. He wouldn't even return my calls. I felt like such a chump. I had a complete meltdown and cried in our boss's office. I told him everything. He picked up the phone and called Mike. He told him if he didn't give me the money for my plane ticket he would fire him on the spot!" ◆

How to Go If You Need to Go

Let's say you've decided to leave—for the right reasons, that is. You and your office mate are a serious couple and it's clear your supervisors won't tolerate it if both of you stay. Or you realize you will be better off as a couple if you're not in each other's faces all day. Plus, the one who has chosen to leave has something else to gain by doing so, like aiming for another career goal. What do you say to an interviewer about why you're job-hunting? What do you say to your boss about why you're quitting?

We'll tell you what you *don't* say: You don't say anything about your romance. It's none of their business. Not your future employer's, not your current one's. Even if your boss knows about your relationship, use your career arc as the reason. It's the truth, isn't it? It's a much more powerful way to leave. You might ask for references from this boss for years to come. Do you want him or her to remember you as the great employee who left the company because of who you were sleeping with?

Same with the interviewers you meet during your job search. Tell them the truth—about your career. Explain that you've learned so much at your current company and now you want to use your skills to _____ (fill in the blank). It's always been a goal of yours and now you feel ready to pursue it. The interviewer doesn't need to know that falling in love was the event that prompted you to make this leap. What if the real reason was that you realized after a family tragedy that life was too short to spend doing work that was less than thrilling to you? You wouldn't feel like you had to explain such a personal revelation. You don't have to now, either.

Exercise for the Soon to Quit
Write the real reason you are leaving your job here.

_____

Good for you. Now you've told your secret to someone.

Now write down the plausible alibi you will give the people who interview you and your boss when you get that new job.

_____

Wasn't that easy?

How to Stay If You Decide to Continue Working Together

You've decided to emulate the couple Stephanie remembers from her second job. How do you do it?

You act like the consummate professional, just like Marvi and Gary, below.

WATER COOLER CONFESSION

"all zipped up"

"I work in manufacturing at a large biotech company. When Gary came to work in my department I was like, *Wow, hmm*, very cautious but at the same time intrigued. I made the first move by accident. We wore white jumpers in a clean environment because we worked with chemicals, so any distinction you have stands out. Standing next to him I was thinking, *Oh my God, he smells really nice.* Then I actually said it, 'You know, you smell very nice.' And I had never said anything like that before, especially not to a coworker. From that moment on we were very comfortable with each other. Within a week or two we were dating and being very careful, not letting our colleagues know. We're both Asian, and an aspect of our culture is to be very discreet about things like this. We interacted constantly on the floor so it was a struggle. Finally someone said they knew we were going out and we couldn't hide it anymore. But there was a formality and it's very professional to this day. The culture of the company is that you hardly see people holding hands. We got married and I only moved to a different department because I got pregnant, but we're still working at the same company fifteen years later and we never show affection, even now." ◗

You don't go into one another's offices and close the door, no matter what the reason. You stay out of each other's professional battles. That doesn't mean you can't share the details once you get home (you are only human), but it does mean that you don't start cold-shouldering an account manager because your honey is not getting along with her. If you find it impossible to stay out of your mate's battles, take this as a sign that it's time for some résumé polishing.

FAMOUS "DATES" IN OFFICE MATE HISTORY

1990 Husband and wife *New York Times* reporters Nicholas Kristof and Sheryl WuDunn share a Pulitzer Prize for their joint coverage of China's Tiananmen Square democracy movement. They are the first married couple to win a Pulitzer for journalism.

By the same token, keep personal battles at home. If you have an argument, don't spill to your best office pal—even if you consider her your friend. That advice, sad to say, goes for good news as well. Don't come in and yack about the great meal you cooked together that ended with the best sex of your lives. And above all, go back and read Chapter 10. The advice doesn't change just because your romance moves to the next level.

As you become more established, it is finally acceptable to arrive together in the morning and leave together at night. In fact, if you are married it will seem downright weird if you don't. If *you* can't manage to carpool together at least some of the time, who can?

Similarly, it is permissible to take a lunch or coffee break together. Just don't do it every day and don't go overtime. You do want to make room in your schedule for your relationships with other colleagues, don't you?

Nonetheless, we suggest you set a goal for yourselves. We'd like to see you handle your office mate relationship so well that a few months from now an office newbie says, "I had no idea you and _____ (fill in your partner's name here) were a couple!" Now *that's Office Mate*-level discretion in action.

── *takeaways from chapter 17* ──────────

1. Go, stay—it can all be good if the circumstances are right. Those don't include volunteering to leave a job you adore for an office mate who isn't committed to you.
2. Don't give your romance as the reason you're leaving. You don't want to say it and nobody else wants to hear it.

PART 3

the global office (mate)

CHAPTER 18

Absence Makes the Heart Grow Fonder

Didn't think we'd find a use for that phrase in a book about office romance, did ya?

But it's just as true for workplace inamoratas as it is for lovers everywhere, and not just after the affair has begun. That's right. Sometimes romance doesn't blossom between you and the office mate of your dreams until one of you actually moves on to another job.

IM from IAin'tQuittin

I can't believe I've read this book so far in and this is where we are. Are you going to tell me I should quit my job on the off-chance Bob in Billing or Mark in Marketing will miss me so much that one of them will decide to give me a call? This is advice?

- -

Ain't, we almost didn't write this chapter for fear it would be interpreted in just this way. We aren't about to say you should quit your job and wait for a love from your former workplace to come your way. Here's what we're saying: If you happen to leave your job for any reason at all,

> you could end up with an office mate from the
> job you just left. That's **why we** put this chapter
> after the "Should I Stay or Should I Go" chapter.
> Because you should think about this possibility
> after you leave your old job, not beforehand.

Again, we're not saying you should leave your job so that the guy who never asked you out will find he misses you and realize he can't live without you.

But it does happen.

Look at Helaine. She wasn't even conscious of wanting to date her now-husband Matt while they worked together. That's in spite of the fact that they went out for lunch, dinner, and the odd coffee break several times a week. That's also in spite of the fact that they usually went bar-hopping together at least one weekend night a week. That's further in spite of the fact that they spent New Year's Eve together, when Helaine had one glass of champagne too many and decided to curl up on Matt's lap.

Not surprisingly, just about everyone in Matt and Helaine's office was convinced they were dating. How does Helaine know this? Easy. At least two people approached her and asked her to please stop lying about it.

Once Absent, Now Fond

So how did they finally get together? Helaine decided book publishing wasn't for her and applied to journalism school. When she left the job, she cashed in frequent flyer miles and spent a week in Hawaii. While lying on the beach she realized she was thinking about Matt. She called him as soon as she returned to

New York, they went out for drinks, and the rest, as we say, is *Office Mate* history.

Except that the story didn't end there. Helaine decided the next morning that she and Matt were such good friends that they shouldn't date. She had never been capable of remaining friends with ex-boyfriends before and she didn't want to lose her best friend. So she told him so. Matt took the news calmly and they returned to exactly the same situation as before, except that they weren't working in the same office any longer. This lasted for about a month, until one night they went together to a party thrown by a friend of Matt's from his graduate school days. After about an hour an extremely handsome man walked in and made a beeline for Helaine. Matt walked over, took Helaine's arm, and insisted she had to talk to someone else—a sweaty mess of a man who kept repeating, "My teachers say my work is no good." Helaine decided she and Matt had to "discuss" their relationship. They discussed it in a cab on the way to her neighborhood and at an empty bar around the corner from her apartment. When the bar closed, they discussed it inside her apartment. The rest truly is *Office Mate* history.

Jeanhee and Luke's history is similarly tangled.

WATER COOLER CONFESSION

"something in the oxygen"

"Luke started working for Oxygen Media a few months before I left. We didn't have many work interactions, even though I was a web producer and he was on the IT side. Most of our contact was after work because we were both part of a large group of young employees who would go out frequently at the end of the workday. I thought Luke was attractive but I could tell he had absolutely no interest in me, which I found a little insulting. But he is also almost a decade younger than me so I let that pass. After I left Oxygen I kept in touch with the core group, so I'd see him when we all went out together.

"I played in a coed volleyball league and my team had a losing attitude—we needed someone with a positive spirit, a catalyst. I thought of Luke because he is such a positive person and because he had once organized a volleyball game for our after-hours gang back at Oxygen. He joined the team so I saw him on a weekly basis. He asked me out to dinner once, but it seemed platonic so I concluded that he just thought of me as a friend. That summer we started spending more time together when we began playing doubles beach volleyball tournaments. At first we lost miserably, but after intensive practice we won our bracket! The next day he asked me out to dinner again, but because of the dinner six months earlier I assumed it wasn't a date. I realized I was wrong when he picked me up during a torrential downpour, completely drenched and holding a flower. I think we went out every night that week and two years later we were married. I found out that the reason our first dinner hadn't turned into anything is that he had asked a mutual friend at Oxygen about me and, knowing he had been ambivalent in relationships before, she had threatened to beat him up if he messed with me without being sure. So he waited until he was certain he was serious. She was totally right." ◢

We know many other such stories. One friend of ours flirted with a guy at work for months without anything happening. She got a great job offer and gave notice, and he suddenly told her how he felt about her. Turns out he had promised himself he wouldn't ask her out as long as they were working together. But she took the job because she wanted the job. It wasn't part of a scheme to make her guy declare himself.

FAST FACT

Which saying has more validity: *out of sight, out of mind* or *absence makes the heart grow fonder*? According to psychologist Robert Pelligrini, it's the latter. When he posed the question to 720 young adults, two-thirds agreed absence was a powerful aphrodisiac.

We can't stress this point enough: you do not leave your job *so that someone who has not shown interest in a romantic relationship with you will come to his senses.* Again, this can be an unintended consequence of tendering your resignation. It is neither a viable nor desirable romantic strategy. It should be a happy accident, as it was for Dan and Isabelle.

WATER COOLER CONFESSION

"to moscow and back"

"Isabelle and I were working for a weekly newspaper in San Francisco. I was the deputy art director and she was the new production designer. My boss tells me he has this new hire who's French, doesn't speak English that well, and that I have to mentor her. And she and I have this immediate dislike. I was this middle-class suburban kid from Montana and Isabelle was this oo-la-la chic thing from Paris in her short skirts. I was twenty-four and she was twenty-seven.

"At this point there's no relationship here at all—no desires, no secret anything. We were all young, it was our first job out of college, and it was a very intense atmosphere. We were an eclectic group of people, this mix of people who would never have been friends but we were friends anyway because we worked together. So as part of this group, Isabelle and I became drinking buddies.

"I had a girlfriend who was a Soviet studies major and she had a chance to work in Moscow. So I left the job eventually to be with her. We broke up within a few months but I had started a company there and decided to stay. Nobody in Moscow had any good marketing training and no computer training either, and I thought, 'Who do I know who can do this work and might also want to live in a foreign country?' So I called up Isabelle and said I wanted her to work with me. I found an apartment for her to live in—it was nicer than my own—and in just three weeks Isabelle shows up in Moscow.

"It's not until I'm on my way to the airport to get her that I realize I'm more happy to be seeing her than I thought I would be. I knew the moment that Isabelle arrived at the airport that we were going to get married. Later she said the same thing, that it wasn't until she was on the plane that she realized how she felt about me. The first thing she did when she got off the plane was to make sure I was single. That night was the first night we spent together.

"In hindsight maybe I had an ulterior motive when I called her from Moscow, but I was unaware of it. But remember that I was her boss. We decided that maybe it would be a good idea if Isabelle didn't work for me. So after a few weeks she went to work for the company next door—they were desperate for people too. We moved into Isabelle's apartment together and we lived there for five years. We got married in France and now we're back in San Francisco raising our two daughters." ◗

There are legitimate reasons to leave a job. For a better position. For a better salary. Because you realize you want to do something else with your life. You don't see "hope Bob in Billing will miss me" on this list, do you?

The key to "absence makes the heart grow fonder" is its lack of intention. Most folks don't expect to find love this way. It just happens. The *New York Times* wedding page—generally a near-primer for finding love on the job—often features such stories in its pages.

FAMOUS "DATES" IN OFFICE MATE HISTORY

1992 The *New York Times* begins the highly popular "Vows" column on its wedding pages. One couple per week is selected for a full profile, complete with tales of how they met, obstacles they encountered on the way to the altar, and funny stories about their romance. Among other things, the column reveals the stunning percentage of couples who meet through their work.

Our favorite concerns a couple who worked together in a dark editing room for three years. They became best friends. But, as the happy bride told the *Times*, "It was not a romantic environment." They didn't find love until the man took a new job at another firm and they got together for a night out. It was snowing and they began a snowball fight. He took her hand. They rolled in a snowdrift. At some point, they kissed.

The story goes on. They dated for a year and a half. Then they broke up, overwhelmed by demanding careers. But they continued to work with one another occasionally on a freelance per-project basis. They eventually realized how much they missed one another and got back together. The day they married, it snowed.

Exercise for Singletons

Think about your previous workplaces. Is there a friend of the opposite sex still working there? Someone who might still be single? Write his or her name here:

_____

Make a call. Meet for drinks. You never know when sparks might fly. And even if they don't, you've maintained a professional contact. It's a win-win situation.

takeaways from chapter 18

1. If you leave your current job—whether for love or money— you could end up with an office mate from your current company anyway. But don't count on it.
2. Love almost always surprises the office mates involved. (Although not as much after they read this book.)

CHAPTER 19

When Your Workplace Is a Romantic Wasteland

- A nursery school with six female, twentysomething teachers and one female, sixtysomething headmistress
- A marketing startup with five workers, most married, sitting together in a one-room office.
- A flower shop.

All filled with perfectly nice people, sometimes of both sexes, but nothing is happening. Sure, there are plenty of workplaces that don't seem especially *Office Mate*–friendly. But the village we keep referring to is a global one, and there are plenty of ways for every working person to use the methods in this book to find love. Even if your office isn't an office at all but a desk in your bedroom. Yes, you can be a lone telecommuter and still find love through your work.

That's because the computer through which you telecommute, the flower shop where you assemble bouquets, the nursery school where you teach little kids their ABCs, are all connected to the outside world of other working people both in your profession and in professions related to yours. Every morning at dawn you have to go to the Flower Mart to pick up the blossoms you'll use for the day's arrangements, and it's swarming with people who range from retailers to decorators to hoteliers and restauranteurs who need flowers to brighten their rooms. As a teacher at the nursery school, you receive invitations to attend conferences where experts from across the country discuss the newest methods for addressing the varying learning styles of young children. Your position at the marketing startup might require that you go to any number of conferences filled with young, single men who basically live in the office and are hungry for dates.

Then there are your friends—both the ones in your town and the ones you still keep in touch with who have moved away—and each of *their* workplaces.

FAST FACT

Pollster Harris Interactive found that 6 percent of American adults have dated a coworker's relative.

You can access their villages in several ways. The easiest and most overt is simply to ask a friend at a promising workplace to invite you along the next time her office gang goes out for drinks after work, but you can be a lot more creative than that. You can network for your career at the same time you network for your personal life. To return to our reference point of journalism, a PR person working at a small office with a bunch of female associates and a single male boss can ask her journalist girlfriend to let her come to lunch at the company cafeteria. The

PR person spies a writer across the room she's been wanting to pitch a story to and seizes the opportunity. If the writer happens to be a nice-looking single guy, all the better. The two of them stay in touch. Why not? They work in complementary fields and the same forces that work in their favor if they were to meet working for the same company will come into play if they meet through work in some other way. The only thing they have to keep in mind is any appearance of conflict of interest, as we discussed in Chapter 13.

Meeting a coworker's sibling is a neat way to avoid this problem—ask Eleanor.

WATER COOLER CONFESSION

"Just one of the gang"

"Brooke was one of my best friends at work. Her brother Luke moved in with her—he was starting a new career as a teacher and needed an inexpensive place to live. Soon he was attending an awful lot of our work dinners and parties. He was good-looking and a bit smooth-talking. Brooke said he did not have a good reputation with women. But I got a great vibe talking to him. One night I went to a party at Brooke's house and he pulled me aside and began talking about his students. I saw this different side of him. He was so caring and engaged. So I asked Brooke if she would mind if I dated Luke. That's when I found out he had been asking for my number too and Brooke had refused to give it to him! He'd gone out with a friend of hers twenty years ago. It ended badly and she was still holding a grudge.

"Our first date lasted eleven hours. For me, it was like finding the guy you had stopped believing ever existed. He was creative and sensitive and he understood and liked women. He says that by the second date he knew he was going to marry me. He proposed six months later. But it was really weird with Brooke for a while. She was my coworker and close friend, and suddenly it went to 'you might be my sister-in-law.' She managed to make it clear that whatever happened she would still be my friend. Luckily, it became clear pretty quick this was more than a fling." ◗

Another idea is to use a friend's workplace to make a connection to someone in an entirely different profession that fascinates you. Call it a work hobby. Many of us chose one career over another, and we still have skills that would have worked for that other career. We might even be maintaining the interests that would lead us to that career if what we're doing now stopped working out. If you're one of these Renaissance workers—a banker who wonders if she should have gone to medical school, say—ask your friend the dermatologist to meet you for lunch at her hospital cafeteria and sit with some eligible doctor friends. They hardly have a life outside the hospital anyway. They'd die for the chance to meet someone who's interested in medicine but isn't on their rotation. There are dozens of unlikely ways your work can lead you to a boyfriend—it worked for Jenny.

WATER COOLER CONFESSION

"sale on love in aisle seven"

"I'm a singer-songwriter, so I spend a lot of time buying string for my guitar. One day I wandered over to the recording section. I was thinking about buying a four-track, but not seriously, and Nick came over to help me. I began asking questions and he interrupted me. 'I am so sorry,' he said. 'I'm too distracted to discuss this. Can we talk about it over coffee instead?' Now, I'd already been asked on four dates by other salesmen there and never went. But he kept asking, 'What about tomorrow night? Saturday night? Monday night?' and I finally said yes. Once I said yes I couldn't stop thinking about him. I came back to the store the next day with makeup on and bought the four-track player. I then went back the day after that, claiming to have bought the wrong cable. He suggested we go out right then for coffee but I made him wait until Monday night. He says it was love at first sight." ◆

Your Workplace Is Not an Island

What we're trying to say is that viewing your workplace as one bead in a necklace strung with other workplaces takes you one step further than the old *take-a-continuing-education-class-or-join-a-gym* method of meeting a potential mate. If you're a woman, when people suggest that you choose a night course that is of interest to men and sign up for it, or join a gym where a lot of guys work out, they're saying you need to be where the men are. And that's fine. So there you are, sitting at a desk next to a yummy guy sitting at another desk while you both listen to a flight instructor talk about what it takes to get your pilot's license. Do you want to be a pilot? And how does listening to the instructor get you past hello with this guy whose looks appeal to you? Because that's all you know about him. He's nice-looking and he wants to be a pilot. That doesn't assume he'd be a good one and you'd happily put your life in his hands at altitude.

But if you're a bush pilot named Maggie in a small town in Alaska with few romantic prospects (okay, we're thinking of the plot of the old show *Northern Exposure* now) and you give the wilderness a break long enough to pick up the town's new doctor and fly him in, you might be onto something.

Here are some other ways you can find love in the office even when your office is a washout:

- Make a lunch date with your friend who works for a *Fortune* 500 company. Eat in her company's cafeteria.
- Do it again next week.
- Join a professional organization and attend its meetings.
- Join your college's regional alumni organization and show up when speakers come to town, especially on business topics.
- Interview for a similar position in a larger organization.
- Meet a friend for drinks after work with *her* office gang. Repeat.
- The next time your boss suggests you be the one to attend that business convention you used to dread, say yes with enthusiasm.

Your global village encompasses the world at large. It includes your office, all the offices around yours, and all the village-like professional organizations you can get involved with to broaden your prospects when you're looking for a quality mate.

By its nature, the workplace village is not only a global but a mobile one. If you attend a convention, for example, the single reason you are there is because of your work. That's also true for everyone else in attendance. That means that all of the *Office Mate* factors are in play. You don't actually work together, but you and all the people at that convention have been vetted by the HR departments of your individual companies. You all have similar talents and credentials. You are certainly successful enough at what you do for your company to invest money in your presence at this industry conclave. (Have you ever checked out the registration fees for those things?) And since you're there to pay attention, not to find love, you have that same hard-to-get aspect that works for you back at the home office, as Addie had the good fortune to learn.

WATER COOLER CONFESSION

"snowboards passing in the night"

"Robert and I met at a companywide conference in Miami. Robert was from the Paris office, I was from the Portland office. We had the same position with the company for our respective territories. There were more than 500 people in the auditorium, but our eyes met and we smiled at one another. It wasn't until the last evening of the event that we were actually introduced. I spoke what little French I remembered from high school and he tried his English out on me. It turned out we were both passionate snowboarders. He invited me to go snowboarding with him in the French Alps but when I told him I had used up all my vacation time, he seemed to take that as a rejection. No hookup for us—we never exchanged contact information and didn't stay in touch.

"Almost a year went by. Robert had a customer who needed help with something a customer of mine was an expert in. He e-mailed me. My heart raced when I saw his name. Could it be? I looked up his profile on the company's system and when I felt confident that this was him, I wrote him—in French—'Do you remember me? When are we going snowboarding?' After what felt like days, he responded. We talked about snowboarding together in France after our next sales convention. On the first day of the worldwide meeting, we arranged to get together. At first sight there were fireworks and chemistry but we couldn't act on it because we were in sight of some colleagues. We met up for snowboarding in France six weeks later and we've been a couple ever since." ◗

Again, enhancing your career and your personal life don't have to be mutually exclusive pursuits. The further along you are in your career, the greater your understanding of the benefits of belonging to professional associations and attending their functions. You should know as many people in your profession as you can, both to learn how to make your own career move along more quickly and to create opportunities for your company. Keeping your eyes open for a personal merger doesn't diminish those benefits in the least.

FAMOUS "DATES" IN OFFICE MATE HISTORY

20th century Famed psychiatrist Carl Jung conducts long-term affairs with several of his patients, including future psychoanalysts and collaborators Sabina Spielrein and Toni Wolff. His affair with Spielrein would last five years, the one with Wolff, two decades, even though such violations of the doctor-patient relationship were widely frowned upon.

Don't Violate Boundaries

Here's what you *can't* do when your office is limiting. You can't date someone you meet through work who is considered off-limits within your profession. If you're a lawyer, you can't date the person you represent. If you're a psychologist, you can't fool around with a client. But even if you do work in a tiny office populated only by people you're forbidden to date, you can still meet the man of your dreams. Karen did.

WATER COOLER CONFESSION

"your place or mine?"

"I'm a psychologist and I do some testing in schools, so I was asked by the superintendent to test a middle school student whom I didn't think needed testing. I found out the child was receiving counseling from Jerry, so I made an appointment to meet with him to discuss the case. As soon as I saw him I fell for him. I was looking for a ring on his finger or anything to indicate a mate and I just wanted to jump in his lap. I handed him my business card and I said, 'This is my home number so, anytime, just go right ahead and call me.' I couldn't have been more clear except to have asked him to dinner. But he didn't call. I knew someone who knew him; she confirmed for me that Jerry was single and that he wasn't seriously involved with anyone. She suggested I go ahead and ask him out. After a long while I called and said, 'Hi, this is Karen and I just wanted to know if you wanted to go out.' He said yes. I said, 'Okay, I don't know what to do from here because I've never asked anyone out before, so if you could take over from here?' So he said, 'Oh, well, would you like to go to dinner?' And I said yes. That was our first date. We never went out again after that—we just spent all our time either talking to each other on the phone or going to each other's houses. After a couple of weeks we decided it was getting silly and we picked which one of our places we should live in together. Later he explained that he's not really good at picking up on social cues from women, and that's why he never called me!" ◗

But let's say that even Karen's scenario can't apply to you. Let's say you work for an office so small or insular, or in an office that's in a town so small or insular, that none of these possibilities exist. Maybe you *are* Maggie, the bush pilot in Alaska. You love being a lone pilot but you hate being single. Should you move to another town? Fly planes for a big company instead of for yourself?

IM from IKnewIt ✕

You guys are so predictable. I was just waiting for you to say that I should quit my job if I can't find love there. I have to say, I didn't realize you would suggest leaving town, too, but don't you think you're placing a little too much importance on meeting someone at the office?

- -

Okay KnewIt, you're onto us. But just wait a second. Aren't you reading this book because you want to find love? If you had found it in some other way you wouldn't be reading Office Mate. And can you make room for the possibility that if your office isn't able to provide you with a love interest that there may be other things it's not providing you as well? An office so small in a town so small that you can't find a relationship sounds like it's lacking more than one thing you need.

You don't have to go to any extremes to take advantage of the romantic advantages of the work village we discuss in *Office Mate*. Put the idea aside for a moment. Does that mean you are going to say no to the next industry conference on principle? Are you going to toss away the possibility of giving a speech or teaching a course to others who want to learn how to do what you do? Of course you wouldn't. So don't do it for love. Do it for your career. Consider the new romance you might find to be a bonus.

takeaways from chapter 19

1. It doesn't matter how much of a bust your own office seems to be romantically. It doesn't even have to be an office—you can still find an office mate.
2. What you're trying to do is meet someone *through* your work. That doesn't necessarily mean you have to meet someone *at* work.
3. Whatever the romantic result of your extra-office activities, they'll only enhance your career.

Happily Ever After, Which Is the Point

There was a time when people who were interested in meeting a romantic partner were surrounded by a community. A supportive community. A knowledgeable community.

It was a community where many people knew things about both partners and their families. It was a community that gave single people the luxury of time to know one another, to go well beyond looks and style when deciding to invest more time in a possible pairing.

It was a community where most people came from similar backgrounds, and they held similar expectations for what marriage would offer. It was a community that made sure the potential partners—or their families—were well informed about one another well before the first kiss was exchanged.

Before you picked up this book, you thought such communities were things of the past, that you were on your own when it came to finding a potential mate. The closest thing you had to a community, you thought, was the Internet.

Now you know the workplace is the modern village. Without meaning to, the modern workforce has given us a way to simulate the community of the past. People's characters and reputation are known to us. Their good traits and bad ones are there for us to see. We get the time to really know one another and to make romantic decisions at leisure.

When we find love on the job, we have embraced a new way of creating community and partnership. It is not always easy, but no one ever said love is easy, no matter where you find it. So remember this: You love. You are loved. Life is good.

As for the rest of you, what are you waiting for? Get to work. You never know what you will find.

Much love,

Stephanie and *Helaine*

Index

index